Corporate Director's Guidebook

SEVENTH EDITION

Corporate Laws Committee

AMERICAN**BAR**ASSOCIATION

Business Law Section

Cover design by Catherine Zaccarine/ABA Design

The materials contained herein represent the opinions of the authors and/or the editors, and should not be construed to be the views or opinions of the law firms or companies with whom such persons are in partnership with, associated with, or employed by, nor of the American Bar Association or the Section of Business Law unless adopted pursuant to the bylaws of the Association.

Nothing contained in this book is to be considered as the rendering of legal advice for specific cases, and readers are responsible for obtaining such advice from their own legal counsel. This book is intended for educational and informational purposes only.

© 2020 American Bar Association. All rights reserved.

No part of this publication may be reproduced, stored in a retrieval system, or transmitted in any form or by any means, electronic, mechanical, photocopying, recording, or otherwise, without the prior written permission of the publisher. For permission contact the ABA Copyrights & Contracts Department, copyright@americanbar.org, or complete the online form at http://www.americanbar.org/utility/reprint.html.

Printed in the United States of America.
24 23 22 21 20   5 4 3 2

A catalog record for this book is available from the Library of Congress.

Discounts are available for books ordered in bulk. Special consideration is given to state bars, CLE programs, and other bar-related organizations. Inquire at Book Publishing, ABA Publishing, American Bar Association, 321 N. Clark Street, Chicago, Illinois 60654-7598.

www.ShopABA.org

Table of Contents

Foreword vii
Corporate Laws Committee ix

Chapter 1: Overview 1

Chapter 2: Joining a Board of Directors 3
    A. Your Evaluation of the Corporation 3
    B. Your Evaluation of the Board. 4
    C. Your Candidacy 5
    D. The Board's Expectations 6
    E. Compensation. 6
    F. Exposure 6
    G. Private Corporation Boards 7
    H. Onboarding. 8

Chapter 3: Duties of a Corporate Director .9
    A. Board Duties 10
        1. Responsibilities 11
        2. Legal Obligations. 15
    B. Board Rights 24
    C. Defensive Actions, Election Contests, and Sale and Change
       of Control Transactions. 25
        1. Duties of Directors Considering an Unsolicited
           Acquisition Proposal. 26
        2. Defensive Actions Generally 26
        3. Defensive Actions in Election Contests. 27
        4. Duties of Directors in Sale of Control Transactions 28
        5. Duties of Directors When a Transaction Does Not Involve
           a Sale of Control 30
        6. Controlling Shareholder Transactions. 31
        7. Protecting an Approved Transaction. 32
    D. Financial Distress Situations. 32

Chapter 4: Risk Oversight and Compliance **35**
    A. Areas of Risk Facing Corporations 35
    B. The Board's Role in Risk Management...................... 37
        1. The Basis for the Board's Responsibilities................. 37
        2. The Role of Board Committees.......................... 38
        3. Direct Decision Making 38
        4. Oversight of Implementation and Effectiveness............ 39
        5. Crisis Management 40
    C. Compliance 41
    D. Disclosures.. 43

Chapter 5: Board Structure, Processes, and Operations **45**
    A. Board Composition 46
        1. Board Size... 46
        2. Qualifications... 46
        3. Time Commitment 46
    B. Board Objectivity and Director Independence 47
    C. Board Leadership 48
    D. Agenda, Information, and Advisors 49
        1. Agenda.. 49
        2. Information 49
        3. Legal and Other Advisors............................... 50
        4. Non-legal Advisors 50
    E. Executive Sessions 51
    F. Number of Meetings and Scheduling of Meetings 51
    G. Minutes, Note Taking, and Board Materials 52
    H. Board Evaluations... 53
    I. Communications outside the Boardroom 53
    J. Decision Making... 54
    K. Disagreements and Resignations 54

Chapter 6: Committees of the Board **57**
    A. Standing Committees...................................... 58
    B. Special and Other Committees.............................. 59
    C. Committee Responsibilities, Composition, and Activities....... 60
        1. Committee Responsibilities 60
        2. Committee Composition 61
        3. Committee Activities 61

Chapter 7: Audit Committee............................... **63**
    A. Membership.. 63
    B. Principal Functions 64
    C. Engaging the Auditors and Pre-approving Their Services....... 68

    D. Overseeing the Independent Audit 68
    E. Interaction with Internal Audit 70
    F. Meetings with Auditors..................................... 70
    G. Meeting with Compliance Officers 71
    H. Establishing Procedures to Handle Complaints 72
    I. Meetings, Time Commitment, and Compensation 72

Chapter 8: Compensation Committee.........................75
    A. Membership... 76
    B. Principal Functions 77
        1. Decision-Making Process................................ 78
        2. Independent Advice 79
        3. Structure and Components of Executive Compensation 80
        4. Documentation of Approval of Executive Compensation 82
        5. Legal Restrictions on Executive Compensation 83
    C. Disclosure of Compensation Decisions 84
    D. Director Compensation..................................... 85
    E. Additional Responsibilities.................................. 87
        1. Areas of Expanded Committee Scope 87
        2. ERISA Fiduciary Considerations 88

Chapter 9: Nominating and Governance Committee 89
    A. Membership... 89
    B. Criteria for Board Membership 90
    C. Evaluating Board Incumbents 91
    D. Nominating Directors 92
    E. Recommending Committee Members and Chairs 93
    F. Chief Executive Officer and Other Management Succession 93
    G. Other Committee and Corporate Governance Functions........ 95
    H. Board Leadership 96

Chapter 10: The Relationship between the Board of Directors
             and Shareholders 97
    A. Director Elections.. 97
        1. Term 98
        2. Voting Standards....................................... 98
        3. Contested Elections..................................... 99
    B. Shareholder Relations 100
        1. Shareholder Engagement by Management 101
        2. Shareholder Engagement by Directors.................... 102
        3. Environmental and Social Issues......................... 103
        4. Shareholder Proxy Voting Advisory Firms................. 104
        5. Activist Investors...................................... 105

Chapter 11: Duties under the Federal Securities Laws...........107
   A. SEC Reporting Requirements............................... 108
   B. Proxy Statements 109
   C. Registration Statements................................... 109
   D. Sales by Controlling Persons.............................. 110
   E. Reporting Share Ownership and Transactions; Short-Swing Profits... 111
   F. Insider Trading... 112
   G. Fair Disclosure 113
   H. Compliance Programs...................................... 114
   I. Directors of Foreign Corporations 114

Chapter 12: Liabilities, Indemnification, and Insurance..........115
   A. Sources of Liability...................................... 115
      1. Corporate Law Liability 115
      2. Federal Securities Law Liability....................... 116
      3. Liability under Other Laws 116
   B. Protections.. 117
      1. Limitation of Liability................................ 117
      2. Indemnification 117
      3. Advance for Expenses................................... 118
      4. Mandatory Indemnification and Advance for Expenses..... 118
      5. Indemnification Agreements............................. 118
      6. Insurance.. 119

Foreword

This is the Seventh Edition of the *Corporate Director's Guidebook*. Since its initial publication in 1978, countless directors, business executives, advisors, students of corporate governance, and others have come to rely on the advice and commentary in the *Guidebook*.

The primary purpose of the *Guidebook* is to provide concise, practical guidance to corporate directors in meeting their responsibilities. The *Guidebook* focuses on the role of the individual director in the context of the duties and functions of the board and its key committees (audit, nominating and governance, and compensation). Although many director decisions and tasks occur against a legal backdrop, we emphasize the law only in limited and necessary instances; otherwise the *Guidebook* attempts to avoid legalisms.

The Seventh Edition explores the role of directors in the ever-evolving area of engagement between a corporation and its shareholders.

Director decisions and oversight responsibilities continue to be subject to a significant level of public and shareholder scrutiny. To help directors engage in effective oversight and decision-making processes in the current environment, the Seventh Edition emphasizes the following key topics:

- the role of directors in the engagement between a corporation and its shareholders;
- tension between long-term strategies for growth and the interests of investors with a short-term focus;
- corporate responsibility and social goals in long-term value creation;
- sustainability and ESG (environmental, social, and governance) performance;
- employee safety, welfare, and talent development;
- board composition, refreshment, diversity, skills, and compensation;

- executive compensation design, particularly as it relates to performance and risk;
- risk management, including processes for identification, assessment, and mitigation;
- crisis preparedness, including natural and technological crises as well as reputational risks from any inappropriate, unethical, or illegal behavior of executives or other constituents of the corporation; and
- fiduciary duties and best practices in mergers and acquisitions (whether negotiated or unsolicited).

The *Guidebook* provides important information for directors of public companies and also is relevant to directors of all companies in understanding their duties and obligations. The Corporate Laws Committee hopes directors and their advisors will benefit from this Seventh Edition of the *Guidebook*.

Respectfully submitted,

David B.H. Martin
Chair, Corporate Laws Committee

Patrick A. Pohlen
Leigh Walton
Co-Chairs, *Corporate Director's Guidebook* Task Force

Corporate Laws Committee

The Corporate Laws Committee of the Section of Business Law of the American Bar Association is composed of active or former practicing lawyers, law professors, regulators, and judges with corporate expertise. In addition to the *Corporate Director's Guidebook* and other scholarly writings, the Committee is responsible for the development of the *Model Business Corporation Act* (the *Model Act*).

The *Model Act*, first issued in 1950, has been adopted substantially in its entirety by 34 states, the District of Columbia, and Guam. In addition, important provisions have been adopted by many other states. The *Model Act* has played an important role in the development of corporate law in the United States and elsewhere.

The Committee serves as the standing editorial board for the *Model Act*, reviewing, revising, and updating its provisions on a continuing basis. Moreover, the Committee publishes the *Model Business Corporation Act Annotated*, a comprehensive compilation of the *Model Act* with cases and authorities relevant to its provisions.

The roster of active Committee participants during the publication of the Seventh Edition of the *Guidebook* (including appointed members, senior advisors, reporters, secretaries, consultants, and liaisons from other ABA committees) is listed below.

Claudia H. Allen	*Willard L. Boyd, III*	*Nathaniel L. Doliner*
Chicago, IL	Des Moines, IA	Tampa, FL
Stuart D. Ames	*Douglas K. Chia*	*Robert W. Downes*
Miami, FL	Princeton, NJ	New York, NY
Daniel G. Berick	*Paul L. Choi*	*Karl John Ege*
Cleveland, OH	Chicago, IL	Seattle, WA
C. Stephen Bigler	*William H. Clark, Jr.*	*Andrea Farley*
Wilmington, DE	Philadelphia, PA	Atlanta, GA

Margaret M. Foran
Newark, NJ

Mark J. Gentile
Wilmington, DE

Maureen Brennan Gershanik
New Orleans, LA

Steven M. Haas
Richmond, VA

Professor Lawrence A. Hamermesh
Wilmington, DE

James J. Hanks, Jr.
Baltimore, MD

Carol Hansell
Toronto, ON

Keith F. Higgins
Boston, MA

William D. Johnston
Wilmington, DE

Judith H. Jones
Hartford, CT

Mary Ann Jorgenson
Bratenahl, OH

Stanley Keller
Boston, MA

John H. Lawrence, Jr.
Hartford, CT

Professor Jonathan C. Lipson
Philadelphia, PA

James I. Lotstein
Hartford, CT

Frederick C. Lowinger
Chicago, IL

Scott E. Ludwig
Huntsville, AL

Bruce Alan Mann
San Francisco, CA

David B.H. Martin
Washington, DC

David C. McBride
Wilmington, DE

James Melville
Minneapolis, MN

Professor Donna M. Nagy
Bloomington, IN

John F. Olson
Washington, DC

Patrick Pohlen
Menlo Park, CA

Professor Elizabeth Pollman
Los Angeles, CA

Kelly Brunetti Rose
Houston, TX

Thomas E. Rutledge
Louisville, KY

Professor Hillary A. Sale
Washington, DC

Larry P. Scriggins
Great Cacapon, WV

John A. Seethoff
Redmond, WA

David M. Silk
New York, NY

Laurie A. Smiley
London, England

Professor D. Gordon Smith
Provo, UT

A. Gilchrist Sparks, III
Wilmington, DE

The Honorable Leo E. Strine, Jr.
Wilmington, DE

The Honorable E. Norman Veasey
Wilmington, DE

Patricia O. Vella
Wilmington, DE

Leigh Walton
Nashville, TN

Herbert S. Wander
Chicago, IL

Paul Washington
New York, NY

Kristine M. Wellman
Wilmington, DE

R. Daniel Witschey, Jr.
Houston, TX

CHAPTER 1

Overview

This edition of the *Corporate Director's Guidebook*, like its predecessors, explores the relationship of the board of directors with shareholders as well as the CEO and other senior management officers. Shareholders elect the directors, who have a duty to advance the interests of the corporation to the exclusion of the directors' own interests. Shareholders do not have the right to manage the corporation. The board of directors directs and oversees the management of the business and affairs of the corporation and delegates to the officers the day-to-day operation of the enterprise.

This *Guidebook* focuses on the allocation of the respective rights and duties among directors, shareholders, and management. The primary objective of the *Guidebook* is to explore and analyze how directors should devote their time and experience to the strategy and oversight of the corporation's business. The *Guidebook* is primarily geared to the individual directors of public companies, or those corporations with public shareholders and a trading market for their shares. The *Guidebook* is, however, relevant to all corporate directors. It provides a guide for the role of the board, as well as the functions, structure, and responsibilities of the board and its committees. The goal is to help directors effectively fulfill their duties to the corporation.

In their service on the board, directors make many decisions on a regular basis. In doing so, they must apply their business judgment based on reasonably available relevant information and act in what they reasonably believe to be the best interests of the corporation. In some cases, a board may even make a decision, in good faith, with which they know some shareholders will disagree.

In today's world, most public corporation directors are "independent directors" who are not employees of the corporation and who are not directly involved in its daily operations. A key challenge for directors is to direct and oversee management of the corporation's activities and strategy in a dynamic and ever-changing environment using effective processes to make informed decisions and provide effective oversight, without becoming day-to-day managers. In doing so, directors must be cognizant of their obligation to act free of conflicts and in what they perceive to be the best interests of the corporation. In determining the corporation's "best interests," directors should have in mind the interests of the shareholders as a whole. This *Guidebook* is designed to help directors meet that responsibility by explaining how they can best exercise their oversight and decision-making responsibilities through boardroom practices and procedures that promote effective director involvement.

Generally, directors exercise their decision-making powers by acting collectively, either as a board or as a board committee. Judgment, however, is exercised individually, and informed judgment requires individual preparation and participation, as well as group deliberation. Effective board oversight results from both group deliberation and the recognition by an individual that a particular matter warrants further inquiry or action.

Corporations are governed by the laws of the state in which they are incorporated. For corporate directors and the corporation itself, that means that the statutes and state court decisions of the state of incorporation will govern many corporate decisions and processes. Public corporations are also subject to federal securities laws and regulations and the listing standards of the major national securities exchanges. The *Guidebook* addresses the federal securities law regime and, in general terms, the listing standards of the applicable market exchanges that mandate specific governance processes. The *Guidebook* does not, however, address industry-specific or other federal or state regulatory regimes, such as, for example, regulations that are uniquely applicable to financial institutions or utilities or anti-competition conduct.

Most directors are not lawyers. As a result, when appropriate, they should seek legal advice to ensure they satisfy legal requirements and properly support the board's deliberative decision-making processes. Although not all corporations have an internal general counsel, the *Guidebook* uses the term "general counsel" to refer to both internal and external lawyers who fulfill that role.

We hope the *Guidebook* is helpful to directors as they assess their duties and undertake their important responsibilities.

CHAPTER 2

Joining a Board of Directors

There is no single process by which directors are selected and agree to sit on boards. Whether initially identified by a search firm, other directors, senior management, shareholders, or otherwise, director candidates typically engage in an iterative conversation with members of the incumbent board, sometimes while the board is engaged in parallel conversations with other potential candidates. A decision to join a board ultimately comes down to whether the candidate's experience, knowledge, skill set, and independent business judgment are a good strategic and cultural fit for the corporation and the board. This chapter outlines the type of diligence a candidate typically undertakes before coming to that decision.

A. YOUR EVALUATION OF THE CORPORATION

As a candidate, you should perform your own independent diligence on the corporation and consider any information the corporation, or, if engaged, a professional search firm, may provide. Sources of information can include the corporation's website, filings with the Securities and Exchange Commission (the SEC), press releases, news stories, analyst reports (which the corporation can provide), and conversations with management representatives. Candidates usually meet with some combination of the chair of the board, the lead independent director (if the chair of the board is the CEO), the chair of the nominating and governance committee, and the CEO. These conversations should provide insight into the corporation's strategic goals and challenges, its business, history, culture, competitive environment, financial condition (including recent changes), potential or ongoing litigation or investigations, make up of its investor base, shareholder engagement practices, shareholder campaigns, potential takeover approaches, relationship with outside auditors, and relationship with regulators. You will want to attempt to determine if there are any particular industry—or corporation—specific risks or other factors that require special or immediate attention. A candidate's objective, independent views of these matters are instrumental both in a decision to join (or not) a board and in ongoing participation and effectiveness as a board member.

B. YOUR EVALUATION OF THE BOARD

You should seek to understand the board's track record and approach to effective oversight and long-term strategic planning, as well as its approach to decision making and leadership. There is no "one-size-fits-all" design for strong and effective corporate governance. Each corporation has a different culture, mission, business model, operational complexity, and risk appetite, as well as different values. You will want to spend the appropriate time learning for yourself how the board is structured and operates based on publicly available documents that outline the corporation's governance, such as its proxy statement, board and committee governance documents, and codes of conduct.

Use discussions with the CEO and other directors to assess your understanding of the board's independent oversight of the management team. Effective corporate governance requires that boards operate in a manner that is both independent of and at the same time cooperative and interactive with management. High-performing boards operate with a clear understanding of their role, responsibilities, and expectations, and in a collegial fashion in which each director is fully engaged. Accordingly, board candidates should seek a sense of the internal dynamics and information flow, as well as whether there are any areas of disagreement among the directors, between the directors and senior management, or among the members of senior management. Does the board function with collegiality and a culture of constructive inquiry and challenge? How has it weathered past challenges or crises? You should inquire about the identity of any internal and external advisors to the board, including the general counsel and corporate secretary, and their level of accessibility to directors, in order to feel confident that the board receives quality, timely, and meaningful information to support its independent oversight role. What is the board's approach to, and frequency of, executive sessions? What is the board's approach to board evaluations and management succession planning? Because directors must be able to work toward building consensus on complex issues in a fast-paced, dynamic operating environment, you should feel comfortable that you will be well informed so that you can exercise your independent business judgment, openly share your views, and engage in constructive dialogue in an atmosphere of candor, mutual respect, and confidentiality.

C. YOUR CANDIDACY

It is prudent to reflect on your personal reasons, ability, and capacity to join the board. Is the opportunity to serve on this board sufficiently compelling to engage your serious interest and attention in light of competing commitments? Do you have sufficient time and flexibility to serve effectively, particularly if a corporate crisis or major transaction arises, taking into consideration the number of other boards on which you serve or, if you are an executive officer of a corporation, your duties as an officer to your corporation? Do you have any conflicts of interest with the corporation whose board you are considering joining or material relationships with the corporation, its senior management or other stakeholders, or its competitors? Are there any personal, business, or other relationships that might give the appearance of an absence of independence from management? Do you have (or can you develop) a sufficient depth of understanding of the business to be an effective director? Do you and the board that you are considering share similar views on the value of diversity of skills, thought, talent, and backgrounds? Does your corporation or other boards on which you serve have approval or notice requirements that must be considered before accepting a new board position? Most importantly, do you believe that senior management and the board have integrity and conduct themselves in a transparent, honest, and ethical manner?

During the process, you should also learn about any directors designated by investors or those with other significant connections between the board members and shareholders, as well as the status of those relationships. It is also helpful to ascertain whether any directors recently terminated their service and understand their views of the corporation and the reasons for their departure.

Although the vast majority of public corporation directors are nominated by the incumbent board on behalf of all of the shareholders, some are nominated by or as representatives of significant shareholders. Nominees or representatives of a particular shareholder should also consider that shareholder's expectations, the relationship of that shareholder to the corporation and other members of the board, and any ongoing relationships between the nominee and the shareholder. Additional concerns and process—beyond the scope of this chapter—will apply in the case of nominees in the context of a proxy contest or proxy access. As discussed in Chapter 3, all directors—including those nominated by or representing significant shareholders—have fiduciary duties to all shareholders.

D. THE BOARD'S EXPECTATIONS

You should also understand the board's expectations concerning your candidacy. Is there a particular reason that the board has reached out to you? For example, does the board expect to rely on any particular professional expertise you may possess? Are there committees on which you will be expected to serve, and when do those committees meet? How frequently and where does the board meet, and do you have any conflicts with the scheduled board meeting calendar? What type of commitment is expected in addition to preparing for and attending meetings? Expectations of board members have grown significantly in recent years; therefore, you should also understand the expectations of the board by the corporation's key stakeholders, including the shareholders.

E. COMPENSATION

Director compensation should be commensurate with the time and effort required and the risk undertaken. The corporation discloses its director compensation program in its proxy statement, and the corporation should provide information to you so that you understand the program and any related requirements, such as ownership guidelines, share retention requirements, or ability to defer compensation. Typically, all outside directors will be compensated in the same manner, with appropriate additional compensation for board and committee chairs and membership on certain time-intensive committees. You should consult your own tax advisor with respect to the form of compensation you will receive, as well as locations of meetings, to understand how it will fit within your personal financial and tax planning.

F. EXPOSURE

You should understand the legal framework that can create personal exposure for directors, as more fully described in other chapters of this *Guidebook*. You should review, and would be well advised to have your own personal counsel review with you, the basic fiduciary duties and requirements for directors in the jurisdiction in which the corporation is incorporated.

You should also request a copy (or summary) of insurance policies available to directors (directors and officers liability insurance, commonly referred to as D&O insurance) to ensure that the policies are up to date and provide coverage to the full extent of the law. It is advisable that you understand the corporation's protections for director exculpation from liability, indemnification rights, and legal expense advancement and how those protections apply in the context of potential and actual litigation or investigations, in order to minimize the possibility of a director paying expenses out of pocket then having to seek reimbursement. You should seek professional advice regarding the amount and scope of coverage provided by the corporation's D&O insurance, the quality of the corporation's insurance carrier(s), and whether the corporation has provided the outside directors with separate insurance (so-called Side A coverage) that is not also available to the corporation. Side A coverage can be complex and is generally insurance designed for directors to receive advancement of expenses and payment for settlements or judgments in the event the corporation cannot pay, due to financial constraints, limitations under law, or corporation governing documents. Because D&O insurance is complex, ensuring that you feel comfortable about how any policies work before joining the board is important.

During this diligence process, you should request a briefing on the corporation's compliance, risk management, and control environment as well as any significant investigations involving claims against the corporation, especially any that involve the activities of the board of directors or any entity with which you are already affiliated. Where applicable, this review should also cover any industry-specific risk or exposure.

G. PRIVATE CORPORATION BOARDS

The discussion in this *Guidebook* focuses on public corporation directors. Most directors of private companies will likely have some ownership interest in or connection to the corporation, its founders, or its owners. If you are asked to join the board of a private corporation or a closely controlled corporation, you should explore the expected role of an outsider on the board and understand the corporation's shareholder base (including any factions among the shareholders), business, reputation, and legal profile. In addition to the topics described in this

Guidebook applicable to public companies, you should understand the directors' relationships with the shareholders. From your diligence, attempt to determine whether independent judgment is really desired and whether external legal, financial, or other advice will be available if requested (and, if so, from whom). You should also understand whether, and if so when, a public offering of the corporation's securities is contemplated.

H. ONBOARDING

Director diligence does not end after a decision has been made for you to join the board; it continues during the onboarding process and thereafter. During the onboarding process, you should quickly gain a deeper understanding of the corporation's business and financial prospects so you can become an effective and engaged board member. Public companies typically have director-orientation processes designed to ensure that new directors are fully versed in the strategy, financial condition, outlook, and material issues affecting the business and its operations, as well as to introduce new directors to a broad range of senior management personnel and provide opportunities to visit operational sites and facilities.

CHAPTER 3

Duties of a Corporate Director

Under the corporation laws of most states, the board of directors is responsible for managing, or directing the management of, the business and affairs of the corporation. This responsibility includes overseeing the conduct of the management of the corporation's business and affairs. In exercising this responsibility, corporate directors have a duty to act in the best interests of the corporation. In determining the corporation's best interests, a director should have in mind the interests of shareholders as a whole. A director has wide discretion in deciding how to weigh near-term opportunities versus long-term benefits and in making judgments when the interests of shareholder groups differ.

A director fulfills his or her responsibility through two primary board functions: decision making and oversight. The board's decision-making function generally involves considering and, if warranted, approving corporate policy and strategy; selecting, evaluating, and compensating top management; approving budgets; and evaluating major transactions such as acquiring and disposing of material assets. The board's oversight function involves monitoring and evaluating the corporation's business and affairs, including economic performance, management, compliance with legal obligations and corporate policies, and risk management. Both functions require a director to develop an understanding of the corporation's business, including the environment in which it operates, and the risks and opportunities it faces. In addition, a director should ensure that he or she has sufficient information to engage in informed decision making and oversight.

Although the board is responsible for making certain decisions about, and the oversight of, the corporation's business and affairs, the board typically delegates operational responsibility to management, who are selected by the board or appointed under its authority. Directors should oversee the corporation's operations and make informed decisions without usurping the proper role of management. Often, this allocation of responsibility is set forth in the bylaws or in internal policies approved and periodically reviewed by the board and management.

Directors, individually and collectively, have various duties and rights, described more fully below. Directors should keep in mind that, aside from specific matters that the board delegates to board committees, the board acts as a collective and collegial body. Further, even for delegated tasks, the full board should continue to provide oversight as appropriate. Directors exercise judgment on an individual basis, and a board's collective, informed judgment depends on each director's individual evaluation and participation as well as group deliberation and interaction. When appropriate, a director's evaluation and board decisions may be informed by the advice of advisors and experts.

Federal and state laws and regulations, case law, and the listing standards of national securities exchanges all amplify the compliance and disclosure obligations for the board and management of public companies. These obligations do not, however, change the fundamental principles governing director duties, rights, and actions.

A. BOARD DUTIES

State corporation statutes define the relationship among the shareholders, board, and management of the corporation. These statutes provide, in essence, that the corporation's business and affairs shall be managed by or under the direction of the board. When the board has delegated to management the corporation's operations, it should oversee management's conduct of the corporation's activities without usurping management's role. Accordingly, the board and management should have a clear understanding of their respective functions in the corporation.

Each director must exercise his or her responsibilities as a director in the best interests of the corporation and must satisfy legal standards governing his or her performance as a director. The responsibilities and legal obligations of directors are discussed below.

1. Responsibilities
a. Principal Board Functions

State corporation law emphasizes the board's responsibility to make major decisions on behalf of the corporation and to oversee its management. Major decisions include those that, under the applicable statute, the board *must* make (such as adopting bylaws and electing officers) and *may* make (such as authorizing dividends). Board decisions may also include a wide range of matters not necessarily included in the statute, such as approval of strategy or developing a new product or service. The scope of the board's responsibilities will vary depending on the nature of the corporation and its business.

The board's principal responsibilities are to select the senior management for the corporation, plan for succession, and oversee the corporation's strategic plan and management's conducting of the business. In exercising its oversight role, the board should be proactive in identifying and addressing potential opportunities, problems, and risks. The board should also serve as an advisor to management, providing ongoing direction and guidance in formulating and reviewing the strategic plan. In all its actions, the board should give significant consideration to, among other things, the corporation's strategy, including its financial and business objectives; its physical and management capacities; its competitive environment; and its risk profile and tolerance.

State corporation statutes generally do not specifically define or enumerate board responsibilities, but the board and its committees should normally undertake the following tasks:

- monitoring the corporation's performance in light of its operating, financial, and other significant corporate plans, strategies, and objectives, and approving major changes in plans and strategies;
- selecting the chief executive officer (CEO), setting goals for the CEO and other senior executives, evaluating their performance, establishing their compensation, and making changes when appropriate;
- developing, approving, and implementing succession plans for the CEO and top senior managers;
- regularly evaluating the board's leadership, committee structure, and composition, including by developing a director-refreshment process that considers the expertise and skill sets needed on the board, along with other factors such as independence, length of tenure, and diversity;

- implementing other appropriate corporate governance policies and processes for the board and the corporation, and updating them as the corporation's circumstances change;
- understanding the risks that affect the corporation's business and reviewing and evaluating the corporation's tolerance for and management of risks;
- understanding the corporation's financial statements and other financial disclosures and evaluating the adequacy of its financial and other internal controls, as well as its disclosure controls and procedures;
- evaluating and approving major transactions such as mergers, acquisitions, significant expenditures, and the disposition of major assets;
- establishing and monitoring the effectiveness of systems for receiving and reporting information about the corporation's compliance with its legal and ethical obligations and the risks affecting its business;
- monitoring and detecting fraud, and encouraging employees to report misconduct;
- being available to engage with shareholders in coordination with management; and
- evaluating the board's own performance on a regular basis.

In performing its responsibilities, a board should be attentive to the following aspects of its duties.

(1) Succession Planning

Succession planning is important, both for unexpected emergencies and for the long term. Boards should develop, approve, and implement succession plans for the CEO and top senior management, including emergency plans for sudden management changes. There is no "one-size-fits-all" model for succession planning, but the board should take an active role in assessing on an ongoing basis whether current senior management is appropriate for the needs of the organization, as well as in periodically reviewing management development and succession plans. This process also allows directors to acquire the knowledge required to develop judgment about the corporation's potential future leaders.

(2) Integrity and Reputation

The board safeguards the corporation's integrity and reputation. The CEO and senior management should take the lead in promoting integrity, honesty, and ethical conduct throughout the organization. The board should continuously assess the CEO's performance in this area, support and encourage appropriate values (including through policies and incentives), and oversee the programs and procedures that management implements to promote ethical conduct and identify issues that may arise (including reporting mechanisms). This board role includes directing the CEO and other members of senior management to establish the proper "tone at the top" by setting clear expectations for ethical behavior and conduct of the corporation's business in compliance with law.

(3) Non-Shareholder Constituencies

There is a growing recognition that, in their decision making, boards should consider employees, suppliers, customers, the environment, and the communities in which the corporation operates. Some state corporation statutes expressly allow the board to consider the interests of constituencies other than shareholders. Non-shareholder constituency concerns are best understood as factors to be considered in determining what is in the best interests of the corporation. Indeed, even in states that do not have such constituency statutes, being responsive to stakeholder interests and concerns can contribute positively to corporate valuation, workplace culture, and reputation for integrity and ethical behavior. Moreover, some institutional shareholders with significant, long-term investments in a corporation increasingly expect the board to consider the interests of all the corporation's stakeholders, as well as the corporation's contribution to society as a whole.

(4) Shareholder Engagement

Increasingly, boards—and board committees or individual directors—engage in periodic communications with shareholders. Similarly, many institutional shareholders with significant positions in the securities of public companies expect independent board leaders to be available for direct engagement. Some shareholders will want more engagement than others, and a shareholder's desire for engagement may evolve, depending on the corporation's performance, changes in management, and industry or market conditions. The level of engagement that shareholders expect varies by corporation and among shareholders. The board should inform itself in this regard and proceed accordingly.

Board efforts to enhance shareholder communication and dialogue require sensitivity to director confidentiality requirements as well as federal regulations regarding selective disclosure by public companies. In light of these obligations, individual directors should understand and abide by the board's policies on confidentiality and selective disclosure. In the absence of a specific understanding with the full board, individual directors should avoid responding to shareholder inquiries or communicating with any shareholders. Instead, shareholder communication and engagement should be undertaken on a coordinated and not an ad hoc basis. This subject is discussed further under the heading "Legal Obligations—Duty of Confidentiality."

b. Director Effectiveness

To be effective, each director should understand the corporation's business, operations, products, and competitive environment. This knowledge is fundamental to a director's ability to perform his or her oversight and decision-making responsibilities described previously. Accordingly, a director's understanding of the corporation and its industry should include

- the corporation's overall strategy and business plan;
- the key drivers of the corporation's profitability and cash flow—how the corporation makes and uses money, both as a whole and also in significant business segments;
- the corporation's operational and financial plans, strategies and objectives, and approaches to further enhancing shareholder value;
- the corporation's economic, financial, regulatory, and competitive risks, as well as risks to the corporation's physical assets, information systems, intellectual property, personnel, and reputation;
- the corporation's financial condition and the results of its operations, including those of its significant business segments for recent periods;
- the corporation's performance compared with that of its competitors; and
- the corporation's economic, environmental, and social sustainability.

In addition, a director should be satisfied that effective systems exist for timely reporting to, and consideration by, the board or relevant board committees of the following:

- corporate objectives and strategic plans;
- current business and financial performance, including significant business segments, as compared to board-approved objectives and plans;
- material risk and liability contingencies, including industry, cybersecurity, and reputational risk, as well as current and threatened litigation, products liability issues, and regulatory matters;

- human capital management, employee welfare, and safety concerns, as well as employee misconduct; and
- corporation control systems designed to manage risk and to provide reasonable assurance of compliance with law and corporate policies.

Directors should do their homework so that they are prepared to participate actively and on an informed basis in board activities. The boards of many large enterprises consist of 10 or fewer directors, and few corporations have more than 15 directors. The active deliberation and participation of each director is important. In addition to attending board and committee meetings, directors should review board and committee agendas and related materials sufficiently in advance of meetings to enable them to participate actively in the deliberative process. Directors should expect to receive drafts of minutes of board and committee meetings in a reasonably prompt time frame, so that they may ensure that minutes accurately reflect their recollections of what occurred at meetings and that identified active items are being pursued. A director should also be informed about the activities of board committees on which he or she does not serve. Staying informed is a continuing responsibility between meetings, not just in preparing for them.

Directors should have an attitude of constructive skepticism. Directors should not be reticent or passive. To be a director means to direct—to participate on an informed basis; ask questions; listen to other directors and corporation executives; challenge management as appropriate; apply considered business judgment to matters brought before the board; and, when necessary, bring other matters to the full board's attention.

Each director works for the benefit of the corporation—even if elected in a proxy contest, appointed by the board to fill a vacancy, or nominated or designated by a single shareholder or group of shareholders (e.g., holders of preferred stock with special rights to elect a director). Directors may consider the interests of particular shareholders when performing their decision-making and oversight duties, but each director must act in a manner he or she reasonably believes to be in the best interests of the corporation.

2. Legal Obligations

Directors must meet legal standards governing their conduct in performing their responsibilities. The baseline legal standard for director conduct is that a director must discharge director duties in good faith and in a manner that the director reasonably believes to be in the best interests of the corporation. This standard generally encompasses duties of care and loyalty. To satisfy the duty of care, directors must act with the care that a person in a like position would reasonably believe appropriate under similar circumstances. The duty of loyalty requires directors to act in good faith and focuses on avoidance or appropriate handling of conflicts of interest. Directors must deal fairly with the corporation if they are involved in transactions that result or could result in personal or financial conflicts with the corporation. A lack of good faith would include (1) acting with a purpose that is known to be inconsistent with the best interests of the corporation, (2) knowingly violating applicable law, or (3) failing to act in the face of a known duty to act in a manner that demonstrates conscious disregard of, or extreme inattention to, the director's duties.

a. Duty of Care

A director's duty of care primarily relates to the responsibility to become and remain informed and attentive in making decisions and overseeing the corporation's business. As noted earlier, a director satisfies his or her duty of care when the director acts with the care that a person in a like position would reasonably believe appropriate for a member of a governing body under similar circumstances. "Like position" generally means that a director's actions must incorporate the basic attributes of common sense, practical wisdom, and informed judgment generally associated with the position of a corporate director. A "reasonable belief" should be based upon a rational analysis of the situation as seen by others. "Under similar circumstances" recognizes that the nature and extent of responsibilities vary depending on the business; that decisions must be made based on information known to the board without the benefit of hindsight; and, in some cases, that the background, qualifications, and oversight responsibilities of a particular director may be relevant.

In particular, satisfying the duty of care requires that directors have the material information reasonably available that is relevant to the decision being made. The question of what information is relevant to a decision is itself a matter entrusted to the business judgment of the directors. Directors generally meet this continuing duty of care by attending meetings; reading materials and otherwise preparing in advance of meetings; asking questions of management or advisors; requesting legal or other expert advice when appropriate for a board decision; and bringing their own knowledge, common sense, and experience to bear. To meet the duty of care, directors should consider the following:

(1) Time Commitment and Regular Attendance

Directors should commit the required time to prepare for, attend regularly, and participate in board and committee meetings. By state corporation law, directors may not participate or vote by proxy as a director; personal participation is required. Although directors may participate by remote means, directors who are physically present at a meeting have the opportunity to engage in spontaneous interactions that occur before, during, and after the meeting, and may be more aware of the group's dynamics than those directors who are participating remotely.

(2) Need to Be Informed and Prepared

Directors must take appropriate steps to be informed. Without sufficient information, a director may not be able to participate meaningfully or fulfill his or her duties effectively. In most cases, the best source of information about the corporation is management. Directors often ask management to be present at board or committee meetings. To be informed and prepared, a director should

- ensure that management provides sufficient information about the corporation's business and affairs,
- request additional information when appropriate, and
- ask questions to ensure that the directors understand the information provided and any action contemplated.

Directors should establish expectations with respect to management's provision of sufficient information in a timely manner. If management is unresponsive or otherwise fails to satisfy such expectations, the board should consider taking appropriate remedial action. When contemplating specific decisions, directors should receive the relevant information far enough in advance of the board or committee meeting to be able to study and reflect on the issues. Important, time-sensitive materials with respect to a pending matter that become available between meetings, for example, should be promptly distributed. Directors should review carefully the materials supplied. If a director believes that information is insufficient or inaccurate, or is not made available in a timely manner, the director should consider requesting that action be delayed until appropriate information is available and can be studied. If a director believes there is a need for expert advice, the director should request it.

In some instances the board may be called upon to act on matters or transactions with significant time constraints. As a result, the information that is reasonably available may vary. In extreme circumstances, the board may be justified in acting quickly upon imperfect or incomplete information if it reasonably believes that doing so is in the corporation's best interests.

(3) Right to Rely on Others

In discharging board or committee duties, directors may rely in good faith on reports, opinions, information, and statements (including financial statements and other financial data) from

- corporate officers or employees whom the director reasonably believes to be reliable and competent in the matters presented,
- experts (legal counsel, certified public accountants, or others) on matters that the director reasonably believes to be within the expert's professional competence or as to which the person otherwise merits confidence, and
- board committees on which the director does not serve if the director reasonably believes that the committee merits confidence.

Such reliance is permissible unless the director has knowledge that would make the reliance unwarranted. Delegation to a committee may not relieve a director of oversight responsibility. Depending on the scope of the committee's authority, a director may need to stay informed about committee and board activities.

Directors also implicitly rely on each other's statements, good faith, and judgment in making decisions for the corporation's benefit. Reliance is particularly likely when some directors have substantial experience or expertise in an area germane to the corporation's business—for example, by having specialized knowledge about a particular industry. Directors are expected to use their knowledge, experience, and special expertise for the benefit of all directors and the corporation generally. It is important, however, for a director not to be overly reliant but to use the information relied upon as one element of the his or her judgment. A director does not want to be in the position of saying, "I voted for the transaction because management wanted it" or "because the lawyers said it was OK."

Obtaining input from competent advisors is a hallmark of a careful decision-making process. For this reason, directors who rely in good faith on advisors, professionals, and other persons with particular expertise or competence generally enjoy broad protections from liability. To rely in good faith requires that a director reasonably believes that the advice is within the person's area of competence and that person was selected with reasonable care.

(4) Candor among Directors

An effective board process depends on mutual trust among directors and a collegial atmosphere that encourages candor. Candid discussion among directors and between the board and management is critical to effective board decision making and oversight. Generally, directors must inform other directors and management about information of which they are aware that may be material to the performance by the board of its responsibilities. Directors occasionally also have legal or other duties of confidentiality owed to another person. In such a situation, a director should seek legal advice regarding the director's obligations, including reporting such confidentiality obligations to the other directors and, in some circumstances, not participating in consideration of the matter.

b. Duty of Loyalty

The duty of loyalty requires directors to act in good faith and avoid conflicts of interest. (See the discussion of conflicts of interest below.) There can be many situations in which a director's loyalty to the corporation may be an issue. These situations fall into several basic categories: the failure to act in good faith, situations in which a director's personal or financial interests conflict with the corporation's, and disloyalty to the corporation for reasons other than personal or financial conflicts of interest and improperly seizing corporate opportunities.

(1) Acting in Good Faith

The fundamental requirement of loyalty is that a director must act with the good faith belief that his or her actions are in the best interests of the corporation. A director fails to act in good faith when he or she is disloyal either because the director's actions are motivated by bad faith or because he or she intentionally or knowingly disregarded duties or responsibilities. A director may fail to act in good faith in a variety of ways, including the following:

- intentionally acting with a purpose other than advancing the corporation's best interests;
- failing to act when there is a known duty to act;
- acting with a conscious disregard of or extreme inattention to director duties;
- acting with the intent to violate, or with intentional disregard of, an applicable law;
- consciously disregarding internal controls, risk management, or monitoring and compliance systems; or
- intentionally or consciously disregarding "red flags."

(2) Conflicts of Interest

A director should not use his or her position for personal profit or gain or for any other personal or noncorporate advantage. He or she should seek to avoid conflicts of interest or take special care to disclose potential conflicts that may arise. A director should be alert and sensitive to any interest he or she may have that might conflict, or even appear to conflict, with the best interests of the corporation, and should disclose such financial or personal interests to the designated board representative or committee and the general counsel.

When a director has a direct or indirect financial or personal interest in a matter that is before the board for decision—including a contract or transaction to which the corporation is to be a party, that involves the use of corporate assets, or that may involve competition with the corporation—he or she may be "interested" in the matter. A director may also be "interested" when a person related to or affiliated with the director has an interest in the transaction that could impair the director's ability to be impartial in considering the transaction. Interested directors should disclose the interest to the board members who are to act on the matter, including the relevant facts concerning that interest. A director should refrain from engaging in any transaction with the corporation unless directors who do not share the conflict ("disinterested directors") or disinterested shareholders approve the transaction after full disclosure of the conflict or unless the underlying action is demonstrably fair to the corporation (and can be so proved in court if challenged).

Sometimes a conflict arises from a corporation's plan to do business with an entity with which a director has a preexisting relationship. Upon learning of such a conflict, the director should fully disclose to his or her fellow directors the relationship and other pertinent information. If the confidentiality obligations a director owes to a third party impair or prohibit full disclosure, a director may not be able to discharge his or her duties to the corporation and may need to disclose the limitation and recuse him- or herself from all participation concerning the matter. He or she may even need, depending on the circumstances, to resign.

In most situations, after disclosing the interest, describing the relevant facts, and responding to any questions, the interested director should leave the meeting while the disinterested directors complete their deliberations. This enables the disinterested directors to discuss the matter without being (or creating the appearance of being) influenced by the presence of the interested director. A director should generally abstain from voting on matters in which he or she has a conflict of interest. Disclosures of conflicts of interest and the results of the disinterested directors' consideration of the matter should be documented in minutes or reports. In some cases, it may be appropriate for a special committee of disinterested directors to review and pass on the transaction.

Conflicting interest transactions are sometimes unavoidable and are not inherently improper. Disinterested directors or shareholders, with full disclosure of material information about the transaction, may authorize these transactions. Some state corporation statutes provide specific procedures for authorizing or ratifying interested director transactions. Those procedures safeguard both the corporation and any interested director and protect the enforceability of any action taken. Otherwise, if the transaction is challenged, the interested director may be required to establish the entire fairness of the transaction to the corporation, judged according to circumstances at the time of the commitment.

A transaction between a director, or the director's immediate family, and the corporation is a "related person" transaction under the federal securities laws and may require disclosure in a public corporation's annual report, proxy statement, or other public filings. Even if the transaction does not require public disclosure, the corporation may be required to disclose in general terms whether the board considered the transaction in determining whether the director is an "independent" director under the listing standards of major national securities exchanges listing standards. In addition, corporations may have their own policies in these areas. Waiving such a policy for a director may trigger a disclosure obligation under the federal securities laws. Each director should be familiar with these disclosure requirements and related corporate policies. Both public and private corporations may need to disclose related party transactions in their financial statements.

(3) Fairness to the Corporation

Disinterested directors reviewing the fairness of a transaction involving conflict of interest or self-dealing elements should seek to determine whether (1) the terms of the proposed transaction are at least as favorable to the corporation as might be available from unrelated persons or entities, (2) the proposed transaction is in the corporation's best interests, and (3) the process by which the decision is approved or ratified is fair. If the transaction may adversely affect only some shareholders, the directors should be especially concerned that those shareholders receive fair treatment. This concern increases when one or more directors or a dominant shareholder or shareholder group has a divergent or conflicting interest. In such situations, the board may need to consider protections for the adversely affected group, such as independent advisors or providing for a separate vote by those shareholders.

(4) Independent Advice

Independent advice regarding the merits of a conflict of interest or related person transaction is generally helpful. This advice may be contained in (1) oral or written fairness opinions, appraisals, or valuations by investment bankers or appraisers; (2) legal advice or opinions on various issues; or (3) analyses, reports, or recommendations by other relevant experts.

(5) Corporate Opportunity
The duty of loyalty is also implicated when an opportunity related to the business of the corporation, including its subsidiaries and affiliates, becomes available to a director. Directors must typically make such opportunities available to the corporation before they may pursue them. Whether directors must first offer an opportunity to the corporation will depend on factors such as whether the opportunity is similar to the corporation's existing or contemplated business, the circumstances under which the director learned of the opportunity, and whether the corporation may have an interest or expectancy in the opportunity. Some state corporation statutes provide that the corporation's certificate or articles of incorporation may include a provision limiting or eliminating a director's duty to offer the opportunity to the corporation.

Generally, if a director has reason to believe that a contemplated transaction might be a corporate opportunity that the director must offer to the corporation, the director should bring it to the attention of the board and disclose all known material information about the opportunity. If the board, acting through its disinterested directors, disclaims interest in the opportunity on behalf of the corporation, then the director is free to pursue it.

(6) Inquiry
Under both the duty of care and the duty of loyalty, directors should inquire into potential problems or issues when alerted by circumstances or events suggesting that board attention is appropriate. For example, inquiry is warranted when conflicts of interest exist; when information appears materially inaccurate or inadequate; when there is reason to question the competence, loyalty, or candor of management or of an advisor; or when common sense calls for inquiry or skepticism. When a director has information indicating that the corporation is or may be experiencing significant problems in a particular area of business or may be engaging in potentially unlawful or unethical conduct, he or she should make further inquiry and follow up until reasonably satisfied that management is addressing the situation appropriately. Even when there are no such red flags, directors should satisfy themselves periodically that the corporation maintains information systems and procedures that are appropriately designed to identify and manage risks and

are reasonably effective in maintaining compliance with laws and corporate policies and procedures.

c. Business Judgment Rule

Judicial review of challenged board decisions will normally be governed by the business judgment rule. The business judgment rule is not a description of a duty or a standard for determining whether a breach of duty has occurred. It is a standard of review by which judges analyze director conduct to determine whether a board decision may be challenged or a director will be personally liable.

If the business judgment rule applies, a judge will presume that, in making a business decision, independent and disinterested directors acted on an informed basis, in good faith, and in the honest belief that the action taken was in the best interests of the corporation. The rule applies to suits by shareholders acting for themselves or derivatively on behalf of the corporation. The court will determine only whether the directors making the decision were independent and disinterested in the matter, informed themselves before taking the action, and acted in the good faith belief that the decision was in the best interests of the corporation. If so, the court will not second-guess the decision and the directors will be protected from personal liability to the corporation and its shareholders—even if the board's decision turns out to be unwise or the results of the decision are unsuccessful. Importantly, the business judgment rule protects only decisions whether to take or not take action involving the duty of care. It does not protect conduct implicating breaches of the duty of loyalty.

d. Duty of Disclosure

Directors should never mislead or misinform shareholders. In addition, directors have an obligation to provide shareholders with all relevant material information when presenting them with a voting or investment decision. As noted previously, directors have a duty of candor to inform fellow directors and management about information known to the director that is relevant to corporate decisions.

e. Duty of Confidentiality

A director must keep confidential material matters involving the corporation that have not been disclosed to the public. Directors must be aware of and comply with the corporation's confidentiality, insider trading, and disclosure policies. Although a public corporation director may receive inquiries from major shareholders, media, analysts, or friends, individual directors should avoid responding to such inquiries in the absence of a specific understanding with the full board, particularly when confidential or market-sensitive information is involved. Instead, they should refer requests for information to the CEO or other corporation spokesperson.

Constituent directors who have been elected to a board pursuant to an agreement or understanding with a particular shareholder may be entitled to share confidential corporate information with that shareholder, as long as they do so in a manner that is consistent with their duties to the corporation. Whether an individual director may share confidential information with shareholders who nominate or elect him or her (subject to selective disclosure and insider trading prohibitions) will depend on the circumstances of the situation, including whether the corporation or board expects that information will be shared and the type of information at issue, whether the sharing of the particular information will cause harm to the corporation, and whether the shareholder has an interest adverse to the corporation. A well-drafted confidentiality agreement between the corporation and the shareholder governing if, when, and how such information may be shared can protect the corporation, the shareholder, and the constituent director.

A director who improperly discloses non-public information to persons outside the corporation may, for example, harm the corporation's competitive position or damage investor relations. If the information is material, the director may incur personal liability as a tipper of inside information or cause the corporation to violate federal securities laws. Equally important, unauthorized director disclosure of non-public information may damage the bond of trust between and among directors and management, discourage candid discussions, and jeopardize boardroom effectiveness and director collaboration.

B. BOARD RIGHTS

Directors have both legal and customary rights of access to the information and resources needed to perform their responsibilities and meet legal standards of conduct. Among the most important are the rights to

- inspect books and records,
- request additional information reasonably necessary to exercise informed oversight and make careful decisions,
- inspect facilities to gain an understanding of corporate operations,

- receive timely notice of all meetings in which a director is entitled to participate,
- receive copies of key documents and of all board and committee meeting minutes, and
- receive regular oral or written reports of the activities of all board committees.

In addition, directors generally have the right of access to key executives, other employees of the corporation, the corporation's general counsel, and other advisors to obtain information relevant to the performance of their duties. Directors may (and should) request that any issue of concern be put on the board (or appropriate committee) agenda.

As described above, the right to information is accompanied by the duty to keep corporate information confidential and to not misuse information for personal benefit or for the benefit of others.

The board and its committees should expect the general counsel, if there is one, to be available as a resource to advise them. Correspondingly, the general counsel must recognize that the client is the corporation, as represented by the board of directors, and not the CEO, any individual director, or any other officer or group of managers. The board and board committees should have access to the corporation's regular outside counsel, if one exists, and the authority to retain their own legal counsel and professional advisors, independent of those who usually advise the corporation. The chapters in this *Guidebook* on individual committees address these issues.

C. DEFENSIVE ACTIONS, ELECTION CONTESTS, AND SALE AND CHANGE OF CONTROL TRANSACTIONS

Defensive actions, proxy contests, and sale and change of control transactions are extraordinary situations that may affect control of the corporation and also may involve challenges to the board's corporate strategy. Decisions implicating control of the corporation present a greater potential for director conflicts of interest than ordinary business decisions. As a result, when reviewing director decisions relating to sale and change of control transactions, courts in many states apply different legal standards than those that are applied to ordinary business decisions. Under these legal standards, the deferential business judgment rule does not apply to director decisions relating to sale and change of control transactions that have not been approved by disinterested shareholders until the directors demonstrate that they are both not conflicted and reasonably informed.

The following is an overview of the fiduciary principles applicable to director decisions relating to defensive actions, proxy contests, and sale and change of control transactions. The legal standards described are based principally on Delaware law as interpreted by the Delaware courts. Because Delaware is the state of incorporation of a majority of publicly traded corporations in the United States, many of the court decisions defining and applying the legal standards for director conduct in sale and change of control transactions have been issued by the Delaware courts. Courts outside of Delaware often apply Delaware legal standards when considering challenges to director conduct and, even when they do not, they frequently reference those standards. Delaware legal standards are not binding on other states, however, and the legislatures and courts in some states have expressly chosen not to apply the Delaware legal standards to sale and change of control transactions.

1. Duties of Directors Considering an Unsolicited Acquisition Proposal

Upon receipt of a credible unsolicited proposal to acquire control of the corporation or substantially all of its assets, directors should review the proposal and determine whether pursuing it is in the best interests of the corporation and its shareholders. Directors are not obligated to accept an unsolicited offer, negotiate or enter into discussions with an offeror, abandon the corporation's long-term strategy, or sell the corporation, even if the proposal offers a substantial premium to the current market price of the corporation's stock. In determining whether to pursue the proposal, the directors may consider the opportunities and risks of running the business over the short, medium, and long terms. The board may find it helpful to engage a financial advisor to assist it in evaluating the financial aspects of the unsolicited proposal in comparison to continuing with the corporation's long-term strategy.

Unless the directors are conflicted or not adequately informed, the business judgment rule will apply to a decision to pursue or not pursue an unsolicited acquisition proposal. The fact that the proposal may result in the directors not staying in office does not in itself create a conflict for the directors considering the proposal. As discussed below, however, if the directors decide to erect defensive measures against an unsolicited proposal or to sell the corporation or substantially all of its assets, courts may apply more stringent standards to the board's decision.

2. Defensive Actions Generally

If directors take defensive action, such as adopting a "poison pill" shareholder rights plan, in response to an unsolicited proposal or other perceived threat to the corporation, the business judgment rule initially will not apply. Rather, courts apply a two-pronged analysis that looks to whether there is a reasonably perceived threat to the corporation justifying a response, and whether the chosen response is reasonable and proportionate in relation to the threat posed. This standard is often referred to as the *Unocal* standard, derived from a landmark Delaware Supreme Court decision involving a hostile bid for Unocal Corporation.

When the *Unocal* standard applies, directors can demonstrate that they had reasonable grounds to believe there is a threat to the corporation by showing that the board consisted of a majority of non-conflicted directors who relied on the advice of legal counsel and financial advisors. The reasonableness of the response is evaluated in the context of the specific threat. Often there will be more than one reasonable response. The board may choose any reasonable response, even if the court or shareholders might have made a different choice.

The board's response is not reasonable if it is preclusive or coercive. A preclusive response effectively precludes other alternatives because it makes any alternative to the board's response mathematically impossible or realistically unattainable. A response is coercive if it effectively forces shareholders to accept a response that they have no real choice but to accept because of negative consequences to their investment if they do not accept the response. In addition, courts will consider whether the response is proportionate to the threat. A response that has a limited duration and maintains the flexibility of the board to address future events is generally viewed as reasonable and proportionate. For example, courts have viewed as a reasonable and proportionate defensive response a poison pill that stays in place for a finite period of time and that can be redeemed or amended by a future board. In contrast, a poison pill that can be redeemed or amended only by the current board, and not by future directors, has been found to be an unreasonable and disproportionate response because it prevents shareholders from electing other directors who would redeem the poison pill.

Once the directors show they had reasonable grounds to believe a threat to the corporation existed and that the defensive action chosen is reasonable and proportionate, the business judgment rule applies to the defensive action.

3. Defensive Actions in Election Contests

Defensive actions in contested elections are subject to a more stringent standard of review than defensive actions in other contexts. When the primary purpose of a defensive measure is to interfere with the shareholder vote in a contested election of directors, directors must first demonstrate a compelling justification for the measure. This standard is often referred to as the *Blasius* standard, named after a Delaware Chancery court ruling involving Blasius Industries, Inc.

The *Blasius* standard applies when a shareholder proposes to take action that the directors do not support at a meeting or by written consent in lieu of a meeting, and the directors act to delay or prevent the shareholder action or to nullify the intended result of the shareholder action. If these circumstances are present, the directors must demonstrate compelling justification for their actions, regardless of whether they believe that the holders of the majority of the shares are voting out of ignorance or that the consequences of the vote will harm other shareholders.

The compelling justification standard under *Blasius* is difficult to meet in contested director elections and in other matters where the directors have a personal interest. Directors may use corporate funds to try to convince shareholders to vote as the directors recommend and may delay a meeting for a short period of time to provide shareholders with information related to recent developments that would be material to the matter. But the possibility that one or more directors will lose the election if the vote is held will not by itself be a compelling justification to delay, postpone, or cancel a scheduled vote. By contrast, in votes on sale transactions where directors do not have a conflicting interest, directors have successfully demonstrated that a compelling justification exists to postpone a vote in instances where they credibly demonstrate that they are doing so not to perpetuate their control of the corporation but to preserve for shareholders what they reasonably believe to be a value-maximizing opportunity.

4. Duties of Directors in Sale of Control Transactions

Once directors decide to sell the corporation or substantially all of its assets for cash or its equivalent, or engage in a transaction that will result in a change of control, they have a duty to secure the best value reasonably attainable for the corporation's shareholders. This standard, which was first articulated by the Delaware Supreme Court in a case involving Revlon, Inc., is often referred to as the *Revlon* standard. Courts reviewing whether directors have complied with the *Revlon* standard consider both the adequacy of the directors' decision-making process and the reasonableness of their decisions in light of the circumstances presented. As with the review of directors' actions under the *Unocal* standard, the *Revlon* standard places on the directors an initial burden of showing that they were not conflicted, were adequately informed, and acted reasonably.

In reviewing whether the directors have complied with the *Revlon* standard, courts will consider whether any of the directors, the management, or the directors' advisors had conflicts of interest in the transaction and, if so, whether those conflicts affected the sale process. Sale transactions in which directors or officers will remain owners of the corporation after the transaction is completed, or in which directors or officers receive, or represent shareholders who receive, benefits not shared by all shareholders, are types of sale transactions that present potential conflicts of interest.

In transactions in which some directors or officers have an actual or potential conflict, the non-conflicted directors should structure and manage the sale process to protect against claims that the process was affected by the participation of the conflicted directors or officers. In many cases where directors or officers have an actual or potential conflict, the directors and officers with the actual or potential conflict are recused from the sale process. Recusal can be accomplished by the involved directors and officers agreeing to recuse themselves from the sale process or by the board forming a committee of non-conflicted directors to oversee the sale process.

In addition, directors should determine whether the financial and legal advisors engaged to assist the corporation in connection with the transaction have any potential conflicts of interest that could affect the sales process. Advisor conflicts may arise from, for example, relationships with parties on the other side of the transaction, parties with an interest in the transaction different from that of the shareholders generally, or parties with an interest in a particular outcome of the sales process. Directors should ask their advisors about relationships or other matters that may present potential conflicts not only at the outset of the advisors' engagement but also as new parties emerge during the sale process. When actual or potential conflicts exist or arise, the board may choose a different advisor or, in appropriate circumstances, "manage" the conflict. To manage the conflict, the directors should discuss with their advisors the steps that the advisors will take so that the conflict does not impact the sale process and directors should actively monitor the sale process to make sure that it is not affected by the conflict. In some circumstances, directors may want to consider hiring a financial advisor without conflicts in addition to the conflicted financial advisor.

The *Revlon* standard does not mandate any specific sale process. Directors have the discretion to follow any sale process they reasonably believe is likely to produce the most favorable transaction for the shareholders. When choosing among multiple cash offers, the directors are obligated to take the highest offer that is likely to be consummated.

The directors may, however, consider financing, regulatory, and other factors that may impact the likelihood that an offer will result in a completed transaction. For example, an offer with little risk to consummation may be superior to a higher offer that has significant financing, regulatory, or other risks to consummation. Further, when considering a sale transaction, directors are not required to accept an all-cash offer in lieu of an offer that includes an equity component; rather, directors may consider the potential opportunities and risks of the equity component as part of the relative values of the offers.

State law varies with respect to the extent to which directors may consider the interests of non-shareholder constituencies such as the employees, customers, and communities in which the corporation operates in choosing between alternative transactions. In some states, interests of non-shareholder constituencies may be considered only to the extent they are consistent with shareholder interests. In other states, however, the interests of non-shareholder constituencies are permitted or required to be considered separately from shareholder interests, without any conditionality.

A court considering compliance with the *Revlon* standard will not second-guess a choice from among several reasonable alternatives. This would be the case even if the court may have decided otherwise or subsequent events may cast doubt on the directors' decision, as long as the sale process was not tainted by conflicts of interest and the directors had a rational basis for believing the alternative they chose would produce the best result for shareholders. Moreover, in Delaware, if the sale transaction is approved by the holders of a majority of the disinterested shares based upon a fully informed and non-coerced vote, the *Revlon* standard would no longer apply and the business judgment rule would become the applicable standard of review.

5. Duties of Directors When a Transaction Does Not Involve a Sale of Control

Not all sale transactions result in a *Revlon* sale of control. Stock-for-stock sale transactions generally do not involve a change of control if, for example, there will be no controlling shareholder following the transaction because there is a possibility of shareholders receiving a control premium in the future. Further, a court will review the directors' decision to engage in an all-stock sale transaction that does not constitute a change of control under the business judgment rule. In these transactions, directors are not obligated to restrict themselves to short-term considerations. Rather, directors may select the transaction they believe provides the corporation and its shareholders the best prospects for growth and value enhancement over the long term and may reject other available transactions even if they offer higher short-term value.

6. Controlling Shareholder Transactions

Certain types of transactions, such as "going private" transactions, may be subject to the "entire fairness" standard, the most stringent standard of review applied by the courts to sale transactions. For example, the entire fairness standard applies to sale transactions in which a controlling shareholder is part of the buyer group or being treated differently from other shareholders. The entire fairness standard also applies when a majority of the selling corporation's directors have business, financial, or other material relationships with the buyer. Courts view these transactions as presenting an inherent conflict between the personal interests of the controller or the conflicted directors and their fiduciary duties to the other shareholders. As a result, the normal presumptions that attach to business decisions made by disinterested directors do not apply, and the controlling shareholder and/or conflicted directors must demonstrate the "entire fairness" of the transaction's terms. The entire fairness standard considers the fairness of the price paid in the transaction and the process by which the price was determined. In practice, controlling shareholders have had difficulty convincing courts that a going private or other conflicted transaction was entirely fair to the minority shareholders.

A controlling shareholder may, however, avoid application of the entire fairness standard to a going private or other conflicted transaction by making clear at the outset that its willingness to engage in the transaction is conditioned on approval by both a committee of disinterested directors and the holders of a majority of the shares not held by the controller and its affiliates or the corporation's executive officers. A going private or other conflicted transaction that is both negotiated by a committee of disinterested directors and subject to fully informed disinterested shareholder approval will be reviewed under the business judgment rule rather than the entire fairness standard if the special committee has the power and information necessary to act independently from the controller and if the disinterested stockholder vote is fully informed and not coerced. By contrast, the negotiation of the going private or other conflicted transaction by *either* a special committee of disinterested directors *or* the approval of the going private transaction by a majority of the shareholders unaffiliated with the controller, *but not both*, may result in the shareholder challenging the transaction having to prove the entire fairness of the transaction instead of the controller and/or the conflicted directors. The transaction, however, will remain subject to entire fairness review.

If the controlling shareholder is selling to a third party in a sale transaction and is receiving the same consideration as other shareholders, there is normally no conflict between the interests of the controller and those of the minority shareholders. Thus, the entire fairness standard normally will not apply and the transaction will be reviewed under the *Revlon* standard for sale of control transactions described above.

7. Protecting an Approved Transaction

The board's duties under the *Revlon* standard do not end with the signing of a merger or sale agreement. Until shareholders approve the agreement, directors must consider any superior proposals and other developments that affect the directors' initial recommendation that shareholders vote in favor of the transaction.

Many merger and sale agreements contain so-called deal protection provisions limiting the right of the directors to solicit alternative proposals, respond to competing proposals, or change their recommendation that shareholders vote in favor of the transaction. Deal protection provisions are subject to the *Unocal* standard for defensive actions described above. Courts have generally found such provisions to be consistent with the *Unocal* standard, as long as directors can consider post-signing developments that occur prior to the shareholder vote and make accurate disclosure to shareholders regarding the board's recommendation of the original transaction in light of the post-signing developments. In addition, many merger and sale agreements contain provisions requiring that a termination fee be paid to the buyer if the directors change their recommendation to shareholders or terminate the agreement in order to accept a superior transaction. The purpose of this fee is to compensate the buyer for its time and effort in reaching the original agreement and effectively set a floor for a potential superior transaction. Although Delaware courts have cautioned that each termination fee must be tested in the context of the specific transaction, they have routinely found that termination fees in the range of 2–3 percent of the equity value of the transaction meet the *Unocal* standard.

D. FINANCIAL DISTRESS SITUATIONS

Directors of a corporation in financial distress may have obligations and face issues not encountered by directors of financially healthy companies. Although the directors' fiduciary duties to the corporation and its shareholders continue to apply in financial distress situations, when a corporation is insolvent, both creditors and shareholders may enforce the duties. The theory for including creditors among the stakeholders that can enforce fiduciary duties is that, at the point of insolvency, the creditors are the true residual owners of the corporation. Because the risk-taking profiles of creditors and shareholders may be different, and because directors are often shareholders, directors of insolvent companies may face claims from creditors asserting that the directors were conflicted in making business decisions that benefit shareholders but that disadvantage the creditors. Conversely, directors may face claims from shareholders who assert that the directors made business decisions that were too conservative and undervalued the corporation, and that benefited creditors to the detriment of shareholders.

Exactly when a corporation is considered to be insolvent, and thus exactly when the directors' fiduciary duties may be enforced by creditors, can be uncertain. In some states, including Delaware, the courts have adopted a bright line insolvency test. By contrast, some states require only that the corporation be in the "zone of insolvency" for fiduciary duties to expand to creditors. Even in states where a bright line insolvency test is applicable, the point in time when the corporation becomes insolvent can be debated. A corporation generally is considered insolvent when the fair value of the corporation's liabilities exceeds the fair value of its assets, or when the corporation cannot pay its debts when they come due in the ordinary course. Because the exact time when insolvency occurs may be ascertainable only in hindsight, directors should be alert to circumstances raising the possibility of insolvency.

Insolvency generally gives additional legal protections to creditors. The U.S. Bankruptcy Code and state law permit a corporation to avoid certain transactions that prejudice the corporation's ability to pay its creditors. Any party, including any shareholder or creditor, who receives a transfer from a corporation in financial distress may have to return the transferred property if the party did not pay reasonably equivalent value in return. In addition, the U.S. Bankruptcy Code permits an insolvent corporation to recover payments made on account of the obligations owed to some creditors in preference to those owed to other creditors. Finally, the U.S. Bankruptcy Code and state law permit the corporation to avoid any transfer made with actual intent to defraud creditors, regardless of whether the corporation is insolvent or the transferee paid reasonably equivalent value.

Directors who approve corporate actions violating the laws governing transfers of assets by financially distressed entities may be subject to claims of breach of fiduciary duty by creditors or shareholders. Further, under the laws of many states, directors may be personally liable to the corporation or its creditors for dividends or other distributions made to shareholders, or for amounts paid in share repurchases, while the corporation is insolvent. State law generally prohibits the corporation from providing directors with exculpation or indemnification for this liability. On the other hand, most state laws also provide directors protection against this liability, assuming several conditions are met. Generally, this protection would apply to a director who relied in good faith on the records of the corporation or on reports or opinions of an officer or outside expert as to the fair value of the corporation's assets and liabilities. And, the protection would apply even if it is determined later that the corporation did not have sufficient lawful funds for the dividend or repurchase. Accordingly, directors considering extraordinary dividends or stock repurchases, or considering dividends or repurchases at a time when the value of its assets are in question, often request a solvency opinion from an independent financial advisory firm prior to authorizing the dividend or share repurchase.

In financial distress situations, directors should be alert to actions or transactions that could present a conflict between the interests of creditors and those of shareholders. For example, creditors have claimed that directors favored shareholders by continuing to allow a declining business to operate in the unreasonable hope of a possible turnaround, thus consuming assets that otherwise would have been available to repay creditors. Conversely, when valuable assets are sold or the entire business is sold or liquidated at a price where all the proceeds are distributed to creditors, shareholders may claim that the directors favored the creditors by selling the assets prematurely at depressed prices and by ceasing to make investments that could have created value for shareholders. These types of claims underscore the importance of non-conflicted director decisions focused on the overall best interests of the corporation and considering any potential divergence in the interests of shareholders and creditors.

CHAPTER 4

Risk Oversight and Compliance

Risk management and legal compliance are critical components of the board's responsibility for oversight of the corporation's business and affairs. As businesses and the legal requirements under which they operate become ever more complex, the pace of business change continues to accelerate, and reliance on technology increases, the stakes involved in effectively managing risk and ensuring legal compliance only increase. Well-publicized financial, operational, legal, and security failures in recent years have led to a heightened focus on the role of the board in oversight of risk management and legal compliance. Second-guessing of the effectiveness of boards from investors, legal authorities, and media is a common occurrence. Risk is, of course, inherent in profit-making activity, and the board plays an essential role in determining a corporation's tolerance for risk, overseeing its risk management and legal compliance programs. The board's primary role in risk management and compliance is to oversee management's establishment and implementation of a framework designed to enable the corporation to achieve its financial and strategic objectives. Effective board oversight also sets the proper compliance culture and "tone at the top" regarding tolerance for risk and can properly align incentives with desired behavior.

A. AREAS OF RISK FACING CORPORATIONS

An understanding of the material internal and external risks potentially affecting a corporation is essential. A thorough comprehension of relevant contingencies, threats, and vulnerabilities enables the board to establish the corporation's risk/reward appetite. Risks affecting corporations have common themes and elements that typically fall into three general categories: business, legal, and reputational.

As an initial matter, assessment of business risks is a critical part of corporate strategy, and risk choices can enhance or hinder a corporation's ability to achieve its financial and strategic objectives. Selecting a strategy necessarily involves an assessment of not only its risks but also the risks of alternate strategies. In addition to strategic risks, corporations face many day-to-day risks affecting operations and financial results. Examples of specific business risks that corporations commonly face include those associated with inadequate internal controls, physical and data security, product quality and performance, management succession, intellectual property protection, natural disasters, and national and global political uncertainty.

The increasing prominence of technology in business and in the lives of employees, customers, suppliers, and others with whom the business interacts has exponentially increased cybersecurity risk for virtually all corporations. Technology dependence has significantly raised the stakes for corporations in the event of technology failures and security breaches and increasingly sophisticated cyber-crime schemes. Security breaches, data theft, loss of proprietary or commercially sensitive information, and infrastructure damage have the ability to cripple a business and result in significant financial losses and reputational damage. Cybersecurity risk is also an increasing focus of regulators and investors. Although virtually all corporations face cyber risks, some companies are more exposed than others. For example, corporations with access to large amounts of personal consumer information may be especially tempting targets for data theft.

Legal risks occur both in the context of legal and regulatory compliance and when failing to manage business risks that may result in liability. As with business risks, the nature of a corporation's operations affects its exposure to legal risks. For example, a corporation operating in foreign jurisdictions may be exposed to issues such as nationalization or anti-corruption laws.

Reputational threats arise any time a failure of risk management occurs. The omnipresence and real-time nature of the news cycle and social media mean that any risk management failure may quickly become public and create serious reputational damage to the corporation. As an example, inappropriate or unlawful conduct by executives, including sexual harassment and personal use of corporate assets, presents an especially inviting topic for news media.

Business, legal, and reputational risks to the enterprise are interrelated. For example, a failure of a corporation's internal controls can result in a misstatement of revenues, a requirement to restate its financial statements, possible disciplinary actions, and associated negative publicity and litigation. Thus, a business failure can lead to a violation of law and then to a threat to the corporation's reputation and legal profile.

Health, safety, environmental protection, product safety, and human rights issues are not only matters of legal compliance; they are also matters of legitimate public concern with important implications for the long-term success of the corporation. These issues increasingly drive consumer and investor behavior, business partner decisions, employee morale, and business reputation. For example, global climate change concerns, the advantages of being a green company, or concerns involving human trafficking, conflict minerals, or similar global human rights issues may affect business reputation, culture, morale, and financial performance.

B. THE BOARD'S ROLE IN RISK MANAGEMENT

Risk management is a multifaceted process that includes identifying and assessing risks, considering mitigating factors, implementing risk controls, and monitoring. The board's responsibility with respect to risk management encompasses both direct decisions about matters such as strategy and risk tolerance and oversight and monitoring implementation of those decisions and the effectiveness of the corporation's compliance programs. The board also plays an important role in establishing and communicating the corporation's risk culture, setting expectations relating to risk, and establishing consequences for failures in risk management.

1. The Basis for the Board's Responsibilities

As explained in Chapter 3, the duties of a corporate board are governed by state law and encompass both direct decision making and oversight. Both of these responsibilities are implicated in risk management and must be carried out in accordance with the board's fiduciary duties. Although many state courts require sustained or systemic failures to exercise oversight in the face of known "red flags" as a prerequisite for imposing personal liability on directors, the risk of liability increases with egregious facts or severe consequences relating to failures of risk management.

In addition to its duties under state and other laws, stock exchange rules also impose responsibilities on the board with respect to risk management. For example, SEC regulations require public corporations to disclose the extent of the board's role in risk oversight. In addition, organizations such as the Committee of Sponsoring Organizations of the Treadway Commission, the Conference Board, the National Association of Corporate Directors, and the Business Roundtable have published guidance for boards relating to risk management best practices. Finally, perceived failures in risk management are an increasingly important focus of institutional and activist investors, and proxy advisory firms have recommended negative votes in director elections after perceived failures in risk management and oversight.

2. The Role of Board Committees

Board committees play a role in risk oversight. Assessment and monitoring of certain types of risks may be more suited to the expertise of a particular committee or may be mandated by law or stock exchange rules. For example, federal law requires certain financial institutions to establish risk committees of the board that include at least one risk management expert. In addition, New York Stock Exchange (NYSE) rules mandate that the duties of the audit committee of a listed corporation include analyzing policies with respect to risk assessment, risk management, and compliance. The responsibilities of all board committees include understanding and addressing the issues relating to risk relevant to that committee's activities. For example, the compensation committee of a public corporation must consider whether the corporation's compensation policies and practices encourage excessive risk taking that could have a material adverse effect on the corporation. In any case, the board as a whole should satisfy itself that there is a clear allocation of responsibility for the regular evaluation and oversight of all significant risks, either through committees or by the full board, and that all directors have adequate information to identify, understand, monitor, and evaluate significant risks.

3. Direct Decision Making

One of the board's most important responsibilities is to provide direction and guidance with respect to the corporation's strategy. In working with management to establish and periodically review strategy, the board should consider the risks inherent in a particular strategy, risks of pursuing one strategy over another, emergent risks that may affect a strategy, and external variables that may change the risks associated with a strategy. In addition, the board should consider the risks associated with pursuing strategies advocated by others, such as activist investors, potential business partners, customers, and other stakeholders. Finally, the board should consider the views of shareholders, auditors, and regulatory authorities with respect to the corporation's critical risk issues. Although the board's role is primarily one of oversight, the board should manage risk relating to management compensation and other matters that are not suitable for management itself to manage due to inherent conflicts or the appearance of conflicts. Similarly, the board may need to be actively involved in risk management when it becomes aware that events have occurred that could be attributed to a failure to properly manage risk. These events could include accidents, regulatory fines, business interruptions, or lawsuits by employees or third parties that threaten material economic or reputational harm to the corporation.

4. Oversight of Implementation and Effectiveness

Once strategy and risk tolerance have been established, the board should exercise its oversight role to ensure that management's design and implementation of risk management policies are consistent with the strategy and risk tolerance. Although it is not the board's responsibility to be involved in day-to-day activities involving risk management, the board should satisfy itself that appropriate systems and processes are in place to identify, monitor, control, and—when appropriate—accept, or seek to avoid or mitigate, risk and to make necessary or desirable disclosures. There is no one "ideal" risk management program for all corporations. A board should satisfy itself that the corporation's risk management program identifies the most significant vulnerabilities facing the corporation and focuses on improving capabilities for managing them in a manner appropriate for that corporation. The range of risk management programs is quite broad, including addressing legal compliance, insurance, and crisis management, as well as core business issues such as industry, strategic, and competitive threats.

The board should also be satisfied that the corporation has both the internal and external resources and appropriately skilled personnel to effectively implement and drive compliance with risk management policies. To assist the board in overseeing and senior management in administering the corporation's risk management programs, some corporations designate a chief risk officer and/or create a high-level management committee responsible for corporate risk management that reports regularly to the board or a board committee.

The board, or an appropriate committee, should receive periodic reports from senior management and risk management personnel about the corporation's risk management activities, and it may want to meet periodically in executive session with the chief risk officer or other risk management personnel. The board or committee should agree with management as to the frequency, content, and form in which the information is presented. Such reporting may include ongoing assessment of business risks, methods and policies for prioritizing and measuring risks, adequacy of risk management resources, and controls and infrastructure relating to risk mitigation.

The board's oversight responsibilities extend to monitoring the effectiveness of the corporation's risk management policies and procedures. For example, a board should evaluate the corporation's preparedness and response plans for a cyber incident, including, for example, conducting an incident response "table-top" exercise and hiring a third party to assess, and perhaps even attack, the corporation's systems and report back to the board on its findings. Not only should the board receive reports regarding failures in risk management and processes for timely remediation of deficiencies but also the board should work with management to establish measurable goals to assess effectiveness. The board's risk management oversight should be forward-looking with respect to strategy, product innovations, cyclical risks, and emerging issues. The board should also be comfortable that the corporation's policies encourage prompt reporting of and attention to risk issues.

The board can enhance the corporation's overall risk management profile by applying a critical eye or "devil's advocate" review, challenging management and others responsible for risk management regarding assumptions and variables relating to risk. In situations where negative events have occurred that could be attributed to failure of risk management, the board should be particularly attentive to management's assumptions and variables relating to risk. The boards of public companies should also review their own performance in risk management oversight as part of the board's annual self-assessment, which may include consideration of internal or external board education opportunities in certain risk areas.

5. Crisis Management

Effectively managing disclosure and publicity regarding a failure of risk management is a key element of controlling the impact of unanticipated events and of minimizing reputational risk. The board should periodically review whether the corporation has an effective crisis management plan in place. It may be appropriate to develop crisis management programs and teams to respond to different types of potential emergencies, such as natural disasters, cybersecurity incidents, product failures, significant adverse workplace events, civil unrest, terrorist activities, or other adverse corporate developments. Good crisis management programs address internal and public dissemination of information, expectations and procedures for escalation of information to the board, provision of backup systems and records, and adherence to employee safety and business operation procedures during an emergency. Board-level monitoring of these programs provides an objective review of management's plans for response, lends credibility to the response, and ensures that board members are appropriately informed. Crisis simulations testing the corporation's response plans can be an important part of making sure that the response plan is effective.

The board's role may become even more critical when a crisis occurs. At a minimum, a crisis usually requires the board to increase its oversight and provide more active support to management. In some cases, board members may move from an oversight role to one of direct management, such as stepping in for management as a public spokesperson for the corporation or temporarily fulfilling management's operational roles. The demands on the board's time increase during a crisis. The pace and volume of communications accelerate, and the need for timely decisions requires meeting more frequently, even daily in some situations. Throughout the crisis, a board should satisfy itself that it is appropriately informed and is proactively guiding the corporation's response. The board should also consider the potential reputational consequences of the crisis and develop perspective on the public reaction to the crisis and the corporation's response. The cost of mismanaging a crisis can be high. The board will be held accountable for the corporation's response and subject to criticism if it is perceived that the crisis was not appropriately handled.

C. COMPLIANCE

The board also oversees management's activities relating to the corporation's compliance with legal requirements and corporation policies. A well-conceived and properly implemented compliance program can significantly reduce the incidence of legal and corporate policy violations. These steps also may reduce the likelihood or severity of lawsuits, penalties, or criminal prosecutions. Although the federal sentencing guidelines impose significant penalties on corporations found guilty of criminal violations, they also provide for meaningful reductions in sanctions for corporations that demonstrate they have effective programs in place to prevent and detect such violations. Boards should periodically satisfy themselves that an appropriate internal process is in place to detect violations and to encourage not only attention to general legal compliance issues but also the timely reporting of significant legal or other compliance matters to the board or an appropriate board committee.

Boards should ensure that their corporations have formal written policies designed to promote compliance with law and corporate policy. They should review those policies periodically for effectiveness and currency, including evaluating the range, depth, and frequency of training and other compliance activities directed to employees. Further, if the corporation operates in an industry, or in specific jurisdictions, that subject it to laws and regulations demanding special compliance procedures and monitoring, the review should be more frequent and intensive. Many public companies assign compliance oversight to the audit committee. With the increased burdens placed on public corporation audit committees, some boards have formed a separate compliance or legal affairs committee. The board or committee with that oversight responsibility should meet regularly with the corporation's business operations leaders and general or outside counsel to be briefed on ongoing compliance matters, pending or threatened claims, and potential future risks. The board should receive reports from management to assure itself that employees are informed and receive regular reminders and periodic training about corporate policies, including those pertaining to compliance with environmental and health and safety laws, anti-corruption laws, proper workplace conduct, and insider trading.

The major stock exchanges require listed companies to adopt codes of business conduct and ethics applicable to all employees, officers, and directors. The corporation should have controls throughout the organization for monitoring compliance with its code and relevant laws as well as a regular program of mandatory compliance training for its employees. The corporation also should establish procedures for addressing violations, including whistleblower policies and hotlines or other methods for employees to anonymously report suspected violations of law or corporation policies. The board should receive regular updates about reported matters and how they were resolved. In addition, all compliance personnel should have direct access to the general counsel or another compliance officer to ensure that sensitive compliance situations are promptly addressed. The availability of direct reporting to the board or a board committee can result in a more transparent flow of critical information to the board and "credit" under the U.S. federal sentencing guidelines. Boards should also ensure the compliance program has adequate resources and authority to perform its function.

D. DISCLOSURES

The corporation's disclosure documents (e.g., annual reports, quarterly reports, current reports, proxy statements, prospectuses, earnings releases, and investor presentations) must fairly present and not omit material information about the corporation and its business, financial condition, results, prospects, and risks. Management is responsible for drafting and preparing the corporation's disclosures, and many public companies establish management disclosure committees with responsibility for preparing the corporation's SEC filings and other public financial disclosures. Although management has responsibility for a corporation's financial statements, the audit committee has oversight responsibility over all financial disclosures. In any case, the board should assure that the corporation's procedures for identifying matters requiring disclosure and preparing disclosure documents are reasonably designed to produce accurate and complete public disclosures in an appropriate and timely manner. In addition to the disclosure documents requiring their signatures, directors should be familiar with all the corporation's significant disclosure documents and assure that those documents convey all material information about the business in a legally compliant and timely manner. Accountability for compliance with disclosure requirements cannot be delegated to a committee, and the entire board may be liable for material misstatements or omissions in the corporation's disclosures. Disclosure requirements for public companies are further addressed in Chapter 11.

CHAPTER

5 Board Structure, Processes, and Operations

Properly functioning board structures, processes, and operations are critical to the board's ability to direct the management of, and to oversee, the corporation's business and affairs on an informed and objective basis. No single model fits every corporation. Instead, each board should tailor its approach to the corporation's unique needs and circumstances. Primary tasks include selecting the corporation's CEO; monitoring the performance of the CEO and the CEO's team; and providing management with strategic direction, advice, and counsel.

Given the part-time nature of board service, boards face significant challenges in governing effectively. All directors have competing demands on their time, and most boards typically meet only periodically. Further, boards of public companies typically are comprised of a majority of independent directors who, by definition, have limited relationships with the corporation apart from their board service. In addition to time constraints, independent directors have limited access to information about the corporation other than what management provides, what the directors can learn from corporate documents, and what is in the public domain. Yet, in performing their duties as directors, they must form objective viewpoints about the issues facing the corporation and the quality of the management team. Careful attention to board structure, processes (including information flow to the board), and operations helps to minimize the limitations of time constraints and information asymmetry, thus enabling the board to establish a culture of discipline, objectivity, and efficiency.

A. BOARD COMPOSITION

1. Board Size

Each board should continually evaluate the appropriate board size to accommodate its needs, objectives, and circumstances. Factors that may influence board size include the need (1) for particular skills, (2) to meet applicable independence or other regulatory standards, (3) for committees to have appropriate expertise and resources, (4) for relationships with significant shareholders and other stakeholders, and (5) for diversity. As a result, board size varies significantly among public corporations.

2. Qualifications

The board has control over its composition through its powers to nominate and re-nominate directors for election and to fill board vacancies between shareholder meetings. Boards need to be prepared to explain why each director is suitably qualified and revisit, on an annual basis, the "fit" of each nominee, in light of the corporation's strategic direction and the board's needs. It is good practice for the board to prepare and periodically update a matrix or list of the personal qualities required of individual directors (such as integrity, candor, common sense, and capacity for objective judgment), and to identify the overall mix within the board of expertise, experience, independence, and diversity that will best serve the corporation presently and in the future. Individuals asked to join a board should clearly understand the business and culture of the corporation, their fiduciary duties to the corporation and its shareholders, and their ability to express objective viewpoints, debate issues, explore and resolve disagreements, and form an appropriate consensus among board members.

3. Time Commitment

Directors must devote substantial time and attention to their responsibilities. The time required will vary considerably depending on the corporation's size, complexity, stage of maturity, and issues being addressed. By some estimates, it is not uncommon for a director's time commitment, particularly for larger businesses, to involve 250 hours or more per year, including meeting preparation and attendance, informal consultations with other board members and management, and review of materials to keep up with changing developments. Directors on the audit and compensation committees have especially significant demands on their time. Certain situations, such as change-of-control transactions, controlling shareholder transactions, financial distress situations, corporate crises, compliance issues, financial restatements, and management succession, may require substantially more time.

Directors considering new or continued board service must understand the scope of the job and weigh carefully the time required to meet their responsibilities. The nominating and governance committee must consider a board candidate's ability to devote the necessary time to be an effective director before nominating or re-nominating the individual. Many boards of public companies establish limits on the number of other boards on which a director may serve and also require that directors inform the board before accepting additional board service or other significant commitments.

B. BOARD OBJECTIVITY AND DIRECTOR INDEPENDENCE

Directors must form their own objective judgments about what actions are in the best interests of the corporation. This obligation extends to assessments of management's performance and the strategies proposed by management. Objectivity and "independence" require constructive skepticism concerning management proposals and the willingness to challenge management, including, for example, by testing management's assumptions.

The major national securities exchanges require listed companies (other than controlled companies) to have a majority of independent directors. These markets also require that key oversight committees—audit, compensation, and nominating and governance, or any other committee to which these committees' duties are delegated—be composed solely of independent directors.

Generally, major national securities exchanges provide that a director is independent only if the board makes an affirmative determination that the director is free of any material family, charitable, business, or professional relationship (other than stock ownership and the directorship) with the corporation, its management, or its auditors that is reasonably likely to affect the director's objectivity. In addition, audit and compensation committee members must meet separate definitions of independence under federal securities laws that are more stringent than the major national securities exchanges' definitions of director independence.

When making annual independence determinations, the board should consider all relevant facts and circumstances, and it should review the materiality of a director's relationships from the standpoint of both the director and the individuals with whom or organizations with which the director has a relationship. The names of the independent directors must be disclosed in proxy statements along with the principles underlying the independence determination, as well as any transactions, relationships, or arrangements the board considered in the independence determination but were not otherwise disclosed. The listing standards of major national securities exchanges also identify certain relationships as always inconsistent with a finding of independence. Director independence under major national securities exchanges' definitions, however, will not qualify a director as disinterested with respect to all board decisions. In reviewing director actions in a particular conflict of interest situation or in a special committee context, courts will evaluate the range of business, social, and personal relationships among the directors participating in the decision or transaction, on the one hand, and the corporation, any controlling shareholders, senior managers, or other relevant parties, on the other hand.

C. BOARD LEADERSHIP

Traditionally for public companies, the CEO also serves as chair of the board. Still, many U.S. public companies have chosen to separate the two functions with the chair position being held by an independent director who provides leadership to the board. Where the CEO or another non-independent director serves as board chair, the independent directors often formally designate an independent director to act as a "lead" or "presiding" director. Each board should decide what is the most appropriate model for its corporate environment and culture.

The independent chair, lead, or presiding director typically works with the CEO to prepare the board agenda and determine the types of information to be distributed to the board and its committees, presides at executive sessions of the non-management directors, and serves between meetings as the board's liaison to the CEO. The existence of an independent chair, lead, or presiding director should not inhibit the ability of individual directors to communicate directly with the CEO. The independent chair, lead, or presiding director may also be called upon by the board to meet with shareholders. The NYSE requires listed companies to identify publicly, by name or position, the director or directors who preside at meetings of non-management directors and to inform shareholders and other interested parties how to communicate with non-management directors. Public companies must disclose their board leadership structure, the rationale for that structure, and its relationship to risk oversight.

D. AGENDA, INFORMATION, AND ADVISORS

Directors should play an active role in setting the board's agenda, ensuring the quality and timely provision of information and access to information, and establishing relationships with key managers and advisors, including the chief financial officer (CFO), chief legal officer, and internal auditors.

1. Agenda

The board's agenda dictates the matters before the board and the focus of board attention. Due to management's greater knowledge of the day-to-day operations and immediate needs of the corporation, the CEO and senior managers often play a significant role in determining the matters to be presented to and acted on by the board. For the board to be effective and objective, however, it must be able to control its own agenda. Thus, the trend is toward increasing independent director involvement in determining the board agenda via the non-executive chair of the board or the lead or presiding director. All directors should have the opportunity to request that an item be included on the agenda.

The board and the corporate secretary or other support staff should prepare an annual agenda of key items requiring recurring and focused attention, such as progress against (as well as periodic reexamination and updating of) operational and financial plans, evaluation of the CEO, and other executive management performance. The annual agenda should also foster the evaluation of board and committee performance as well as the effectiveness of internal controls and procedures designed to address legal compliance, risk management, corporate policy adherence, accounting, and financial reporting.

2. Information

The quality of the information available to directors significantly affects their effectiveness. Because management is the primary source of information about the corporation, directors should insist that management provide them with information that is (1) timely and relevant; (2) concise, fair, and accurate; (3) well organized; (4) supported by background or historical data necessary to place the information in context; and (5) designed to inform directors of all material aspects of the corporation's business, performance, and prospects, including major challenges, and allow them to exercise effectively their objective decision making. Directors should receive information sufficiently in advance of board or committee meetings to allow careful study and thoughtful reflection, and to accommodate requests for additional information.

At many corporations, directors communicate directly with senior-level employees to learn more about the corporation's business. Some corporations schedule site visits for non-management directors so they can observe business operations and speak with employees at the operating level of the business.

3. Legal and Other Advisors

Boards generally look to the corporation's general counsel as the primary resource for legal and governance advice. The general counsel's client is the corporation, as represented by the board of directors, not the CEO or any other officer or employee. For this reason, many boards and key board committees meet regularly in a private session with the general counsel. In addition, the board and each of its committees should have access to the corporation's regular outside counsel, if there is one, and should have the authority and reasonable funding to retain legal counsel and professional advisors of the board's or committee's choosing. A specific circumstance (e.g., allegations of management wrongdoing, negotiating executive pay packages, or a shareholder demand to bring a derivative suit) may prompt the board or, more likely, a board committee to seek independent legal advice. A board committee may also choose to have its own counsel, separate from the corporation's in-house and outside counsel, to advise the committee on a regular basis as to its duties and responsibilities.

As part of their annual self-evaluations, the board and each of its committees should consider whether each is receiving appropriate advice regarding legal and compliance requirements and timely updates on legal risks. In addition, each committee should consider whether it has a good understanding of when to seek advice from lawyers or other external experts, in addition to the availability of advice from the corporation's general counsel and other internal resources.

4. Non-legal Advisors

In addition to employees, officers, and legal advisors, boards often consult other outside advisors. The need for and extent of consultation with outside advisors varies among companies and industries. For example, boards involved in discussions about a merger or acquisition often engage investment bankers for advice. Boards of companies in industries with significant environmental, health, safety, or other regulatory risks may choose to engage outside consultants to review the corporation's policies and procedures regarding such risks. Many board compensation or management development committees employ an independent compensation consultant. In such cases, compensation committees of public companies must consider conflicts of interest before engaging the consultant. In fact, SEC rules may require disclosure of the identity of the consultant and any conflicts. The use of compensation consultants is covered in more detail in Chapter 8.

E. EXECUTIVE SESSIONS

Major national securities exchanges require periodic executive sessions of non-management and independent directors (i.e., without management present). Many boards and board committees routinely hold an executive session at each regular meeting. These sessions provide a forum for non-management and independent directors to raise issues and ideas, such as CEO performance issues, that they might otherwise be reluctant to raise with management present.

If the CEO is also the board chair, most boards designate an independent director, or a lead or presiding director, to convene and preside at executive sessions. Although an agenda may be prepared for an executive session, it is also common for the session to be open-ended, allowing non-management and independent directors to discuss any matters related to the corporation and its management.

Typically under state law, directors in an executive session cannot take formal action on behalf of the board when a quorum of the full board is not present. To facilitate open and candid discussions regarding sensitive issues, detailed minutes of executive sessions are not typically kept. It is important, however, to record attendance and any major decisions made.

F. NUMBER OF MEETINGS AND SCHEDULING OF MEETINGS

The number of regular board meetings will vary with the size, complexity, and culture of the corporation. Some boards prefer frequent, short meetings, whereas others prefer few but lengthy meetings. Some boards schedule one extended planning or strategic meeting each year and shorter meetings during the rest of the year. Boards typically should hold regularly scheduled meetings at least quarterly. Many boards schedule six to eight regular meetings per year and hold additional special meetings as needed, particularly in crisis situations.

The necessary time allotted to board and committee meetings requires careful planning. Meetings should balance management presentations with discussion among directors and with management. Appropriate reports and analyses furnished in advance facilitate discussion at the meeting.

G. MINUTES, NOTE TAKING, AND BOARD MATERIALS

Meetings of the board of directors and board committees should be reflected in minutes prepared and circulated promptly by the corporate secretary or another person skilled in preparing minutes. The board or committee should carefully review the draft minutes and consider them for amendment or approval, typically at the next meeting of the board or committee. Board minutes are the official record of meetings and important legal documents that may be reviewed by professionals such as the corporation's auditors, lending banks and underwriters, claimants against the corporation or its directors or officers, and reviewing courts.

Although there are differing opinions among corporate advisors about the appropriate level of detail, minutes should be sufficient to support the availability of the applicable protections provided to directors by substantive law. Generally, minutes should summarize important discussions and actions, without purporting to provide a verbatim record and without attributing specific words or points of view to particular directors. Minutes that do not reflect that an adequate deliberative process may support an inference that directors failed to consider pertinent information fully, to deliberate with due care, or, in certain cases, to act with loyalty to the corporation.

If named as defendants or called as witnesses in litigation, directors may be required to explain their actions well after the fact. Appropriately detailed minutes may provide a contemporaneous record of their deliberative process and can help when the adequacy of that process is challenged.

Note taking implicates discrete issues to be carefully considered. Directors are not obligated to take notes. Those directors who take notes to help them participate should consider whether to retain them. Unlike the process related to board or committee minutes, notes are not subject to a careful process of drafting, review, or approval, and they may contain statements or notations that can be misinterpreted, taken out of context, or incorrect. To avoid possible dissonance and confusion, many companies encourage that all notes and draft minutes be discarded after approval of the official minutes.

Directors should request confirmation that the corporation maintains permanent records containing copies of the information provided to the board, such as board books and management or other presentations. This information can help demonstrate the board's informed business judgment and assist directors in accurately recollecting past events. The corporation should develop, with board approval, a consistent policy for the retention and security of such information so that, together with quality minutes, there is a reliable record of the board's deliberations.

H. BOARD EVALUATIONS

Major national securities exchanges require directors to evaluate, at least annually, the effectiveness of the board and each of its committees. Board and board committee self-evaluations are most effective when planned in advance, with participants having a clear idea of the purpose of the self-evaluation and the topics to be addressed. The typical goals are to assess the board's fulfillment of its duties and responsibilities and consider ways in which the board and its committees can improve their processes. Many boards find formal or informal director interviews to be a helpful basis for collecting input from individual directors for board and committee discussions. In addition, some boards use written questionnaires to gather information. Questions on these forms should be drafted with care. Qualified external facilitators may be helpful in collecting information and presenting it in a manner that ensures that the views of individual directors remain confidential. Some boards also use external facilitators to lead discussions and provide an independent perspective. It may be useful to maintain in the minutes a record of the process followed and any specific decisions of the board or any committee that resulted, but often it is not necessary or appropriate to retain written materials collected as part of the process.

The nominating and governance committee generally conducts or supervises individual director evaluations, as is discussed separately in Chapter 9.

I. COMMUNICATIONS OUTSIDE THE BOARDROOM

Individual directors often have communications relating to the corporation with management or with other directors. One-on-one communications can efficiently tap into a director's expertise or point of view. Indeed, these communications are inevitable and generally are beneficial to the corporation.

Excessive communications outside the board and committee rooms, particularly between management and a select group of directors, may lead to uneven knowledge among directors about important corporate issues. Such communications may also impair the collective, inclusive, and candid exchange of views at board or committee meetings and interfere with the board's collegial and independent relationship with management. Moreover, because official action by directors can occur only at a duly called meeting or by unanimous written consent, individual "polling" of directors is not effective to authorize action requiring board approval. Instead, the full board or the appropriate committee should discuss issues fully and appropriately at a board or committee meeting.

J. DECISION MAKING

Directors make decisions on a wide variety of matters, sometimes giving direction to management and at other times approving major transactions. As a matter of law, some matters—such as changes in charter documents authorization of dividends or stock buybacks, issuance of shares, election of officers, approval of mergers, financings, or corporate liquidations—generally require formal board action (as well as shareholder action, in some cases). Directors can take formal action only at a duly held meeting of the board or board committee or by unanimous written consent. Generally, unanimous written consents are advisable only for routine matters or matters on which consensus has been reached in a recent meeting of the board or committee.

Before taking or approving major actions, directors should receive relevant information to support an informed decision, including summaries and supporting materials, and have adequate opportunity to ask questions or request additional information. Information is critical to the directors' ability to assess proposed actions. Directors should assure that the level of detail they receive and the scope of the resolutions they approve is appropriate.

Formal adoption of resolutions is not necessary for all board or committee decisions. Some may simply result from a consensus or a "sense of the board," providing guidance to management. Business constraints or a crisis may prompt important corporate decisions to be made at quickly convened special board meetings. A well-developed crisis plan and familiarity with the corporation can streamline decision making under these circumstances. Nevertheless, meeting minutes should adequately memorialize these instances.

K. DISAGREEMENTS AND RESIGNATIONS

Boards usually make decisions by consensus. Acting in the best interests of the corporation, however, does not always require unanimous agreement. If, after a thorough discussion, a director disagrees with any significant action the board is taking, the director can consider voting against the proposal.

Except in extreme circumstances, taking a dissenting position need not cause a director to consider resigning. A resignation should be considered only if a director believes that management or the board is acting inappropriately; that they are not dealing in good faith with the directors, the shareholders, or the public; or that the information being disclosed by the corporation is inadequate, incorrect, or misleading and the director is unable to convince the board to take appropriate action. A director may also consider resigning if the director's point of view is being regularly and intentionally disregarded. Public corporations are required to disclose a director's resignation, and in some cases the reason for the resignation, in an SEC filing. This disclosure, like others, should be done in consultation with legal advisors.

CHAPTER

6 Committees of the Board

The laws of most states permit the board of directors to delegate many of its powers to board committees. No universal mandate exists for a particular committee structure, except for certain actions and duties. Nevertheless, federal law and listing standards of the major national securities exchanges generally require audit, compensation, and nominating and governance committees composed exclusively of independent directors. These committees are universally accepted as standing committees. Reliance on board committees of independent directors to counterbalance potential conflicts of interest and provide unbiased perspective can improve corporate governance and transparency.

The boards of some public companies function almost entirely at the board level and delegate to committees only to the extent required. At others, the board acts as a group only on the highest-level strategy and policy matters and those legally required to be addressed by the board, with most board action and oversight delegated to committees. Each board should tailor its processes and committee structure to the corporation's specific circumstances, including its size, the complexity of its operations and risk management issues, the regulatory systems applicable to its operations, and the competitive environment in which it operates.

Regulators may require or encourage boards of companies in heavily regulated industries to establish committees to address specific issues. Boards may also delegate to a committee matters that require specialized knowledge or experience or a significant additional time commitment. Unlike the standing committees, other board committees may be either permanent committees or specialized committees with a limited duration.

The allocation of specific responsibilities between the board and its committees, as well as among different committees, varies from corporation to corporation. For example, some boards direct audit committees to handle the primary review and oversight of risk management matters. Other boards assign risk oversight to a specific risk-management committee. Still others retain responsibility for oversight of risk management as a duty of the board but delegate certain specialized aspects to the audit, compensation, and nominating and governance committees. Some boards create committees devoted to safety, environmental issues, risk, technology, or public policy.

Boards may also create special committees to respond to specific circumstances. For example, an allegation of management wrongdoing may prompt a board to form a special committee. Another board, however, might assign the investigation to its audit committee, particularly if the allegations relate to financial, accounting, or internal control issues.

As this discussion makes clear, statements in this *Guidebook* that particular committees consider certain matters are generalizations. Each board must consider its circumstances and tailor its structure and allocation of responsibilities accordingly (being mindful, of course, of applicable SEC rules and listing standards of major national securities exchanges).

Directors serving on board committees are subject to the same duties of due care and loyalty and are entitled to the same protections of the business judgment rule as they are when acting as members of the board. Delegation of a given responsibility to a committee does not relieve the board of ultimate responsibility for oversight of the corporation. Directors may, however, rely in good faith upon the efforts of the committees to which they delegate matters. At the same time, in accord with their obligation to provide oversight, boards should ensure that committees establish appropriate procedures, including keeping minutes and records and providing a regular flow of reports and information to the board to ensure that all directors are kept abreast of each committee's activities and significant decisions.

A. STANDING COMMITTEES

In addition to the committees mandated by federal law and listing standards of major national securities exchanges (the audit, compensation, and nominating and governance committees, which are discussed in Chapters 7, 8, and 9, respectively), a board may decide to establish other standing committees to oversee ongoing matters, such as risk management or management of complex regulatory mechanisms. A key factor to consider in creating a standing committee is whether it is more efficient and effective than not for a subset of the full board to develop an understanding of the relevant topic and to use that expertise to review and monitor the issues in that area.

Historically, many public corporation boards appointed standing executive committees comprising directors who were usually officers or who were otherwise available to meet on short notice to address matters between regular meetings of the board. With the increased emphasis on the role played by independent directors, extensive use of executive committees has waned, particularly when they may be perceived as subordinating the roles of independent directors.

B. SPECIAL AND OTHER COMMITTEES

From time to time, a board may need to create a committee to undertake a specific project or responsibility. In those instances, defining the scope of delegated authority and responsibility of the committee is important. The board should consider and establish in a detailed resolution or committee charter the committee's authority and responsibility. For example, a board may decide to form a special committee of disinterested directors to consider transactions involving conflicts of interest between the corporation and its officers. The members of this type of special committee should be disinterested in the subject matter and otherwise able to exercise independent judgment. The committee should also establish procedures for its deliberations. A properly constituted and operating special committee of independent directors may reduce the risk of a successful challenge to the board's actions and the potential for director liability.

A public corporation board may also form a special committee of independent, disinterested directors to conduct investigations involving potential litigation or wrongdoing. In these cases, the board usually authorizes the committee to engage independent legal counsel and other advisors to help the committee investigate the facts and determine appropriate action. The exact scope of authority and functions of the committee will depend on the unique circumstances of the committee's charge, including the credibility of the allegations, the nature of the alleged wrongdoing, and the familiarity of the committee members with the issues. Depending on the scope of authority delegated to the committee, the committee should complete the investigation and then take appropriate action on behalf of the board or recommend an appropriate course of action to the board of directors.

If allowed under state law, a board occasionally may desire to create a single-person committee. For example, a board may need to react quickly to market conditions and delegate to a one-member committee the authority to price a securities offering within parameters previously established by the board. Other than in limited contexts, single-person committees are not ideal because courts may view such committees as reflecting a less robust process and consequently apply a higher level of scrutiny.

C. COMMITTEE RESPONSIBILITIES, COMPOSITION, AND ACTIVITIES

Committee responsibilities, composition, and activities vary from corporation to corporation. Below are general guidelines for each area.

1. Committee Responsibilities

Each committee's scope of responsibility should be tailored to the matters being delegated to that committee. Federal regulations and listing standards of major national securities exchanges require specific duties, responsibilities, and powers to be assigned to specific committees, such as the audit and compensation committees. In addition, the scope of authority and the duties of committees responsible for audit, compensation, and nominating and governance matters must be specified in written charters. Delegation to a special committee may be accomplished through board resolutions rather than a formal charter. The board should give due consideration to defining the scope of the committee's responsibilities and authority, including

- defining the subjects the committee should address;
- determining the committee's scope of authority (e.g., whether the committee is empowered to act on behalf of the board or whether the committee is to recommend action to the board);
- ensuring appropriate independence, including the authority to engage independent legal counsel and other advisors at the corporation's expense;
- establishing standards for committee operations, including frequency of meetings;
- ensuring regular reporting to the board (except in the case of certain special committees); and
- determining whether a committee should be a standing or a special committee.

2. Committee Composition

The board should select committee members using criteria appropriate to the committee's purpose and in compliance with any applicable laws and listing standards of any applicable national securities exchange. Under most state statutes, each member of a board committee must be a duly elected or appointed member of the board of directors. Committee membership criteria may include

- experience relevant to committee responsibilities,
- subject matter expertise that will assist the committee in its work,
- ability to meet requisite time commitments,
- disinterest in the committee's subject matter,
- refreshment and diversity, and
- independence from management.

3. Committee Activities
a. Reporting to the Board

Board committees should regularly inform the board of their activities. Generally, standing committees should provide reports at regularly scheduled board meetings and make available to all directors committee agendas, minutes, and written reports, subject to considerations such as the need to protect sensitive information, contractual confidentiality requirements, privacy rights, and governmental security clearance requirements.

b. Legal Limits of Authority

Boards and committees must take care to observe applicable limits on their authority. For example, most state corporation statutes require that the board, rather than a committee of the board, approve proposed amendments to the corporation's articles or certificate of incorporation and similarly require that bylaws (other than those adopted by shareholders) be adopted by the board, rather than by a committee of the board.

c. Periodic Review by the Board

The board or an appropriate committee of the board, such as the nominating and corporate governance committee, should periodically review the responsibilities assigned to each committee and consider whether the assignments of duties and responsibilities continue to be appropriate and consistent with the corporation's needs and objectives.

d. Committee Self-assessment

It is customary for standing committees to evaluate annually their performance. Depending on the corporation and the committee, the format used may include one or more of a written survey; interviews of committee members, key members of management, and the external auditor; or an executive session discussion.

CHAPTER 7

Audit Committee

The audit committee is critical to the corporate governance structure; in fact, its existence and some of its functions are legally mandated. It has general oversight responsibility for the corporation's financial reporting process and internal controls. For public companies, it also has the exclusive responsibility for retaining and overseeing the performance, independence, and compensation of the corporation's external auditor. The audit committee serves as a forum in which the internal and external auditors, as well as the corporation's legal counsel and its compliance and ethics personnel, can candidly report and discuss issues relating to accounting, auditing, financial reporting, risk management, legal, compliance, and ethical matters.

A. MEMBERSHIP

Public corporation audit committees must consist solely of directors who satisfy the independence requirements of both the corporation's national securities exchange listing standards and the federal securities laws. Generally, audit committee members may not receive any compensation from the corporation, such as consulting, advisory, or similar fees, other than their compensation for serving as directors and committee members.

The major national securities exchanges require that the audit committee have at least three members. Typically audit committees consist of three to five independent directors. The major national securities exchanges also require that all committee members be financially literate, and at least one audit committee member must have accounting or financial management experience.

In addition, under the Sarbanes-Oxley Act, a public corporation must disclose whether any member of its audit committee qualifies as an "audit committee financial expert," a term defined by SEC rules and focused on accounting and auditing knowledge and experience. There are detailed requirements for that designation. If the committee does not have such an expert, the corporation must disclose why. If the board determines that a committee member qualifies as an audit committee financial expert, the corporation must disclose the name of the member and state whether that expert is independent. Because of this disclosure requirement, most public companies have at least one audit committee member who qualifies as an audit committee financial expert. Directors who are designated as audit committee financial experts should be personally satisfied that they meet those requirements.

Audit committee members should have a sufficient understanding of financial reporting and internal control principles to provide oversight for both. New audit committee members should become familiar with key financial issues, critical accounting policies, and accounting practices in the industry or industries in which their corporation operates. All committee members should be current in their knowledge of these matters through professional experience or continuing education provided by the corporation's accounting staff or third-party service providers.

B. PRINCIPAL FUNCTIONS

Federal securities laws and major national securities exchange listing standards establish many of the audit committee's duties and responsibilities. Audit committees assume other functions as a matter of good practice. Current regulatory requirements for public companies mandate a formal, written charter for the audit committee specifying its duties and responsibilities. The committee must review the charter annually. The corporation must either publish the charter on its website and disclose the website address or, at least once every three years, include the charter as an exhibit in its proxy statement.

Audit committee members should understand the tasks in the charter and develop a schedule for performing those tasks. Audit committees generally rely on management for information, including the corporation's accounting, finance, treasury, internal audit, and legal staff, as well as the corporation's external auditor. The committee also has the authority to employ its own accountants, attorneys, or other advisors, and the federal securities law requires the corporation to pay for these advisors. In light of their significant responsibilities, audit committees of public companies often consult with legal counsel to ensure they meet their responsibilities. Identifying the types of information they should receive and review; developing operational procedures and an annual schedule of tasks; and fulfilling disclosure, accounting, and internal control oversight responsibilities are key to audit committee effectiveness.

Although listing standards vary, the following list sets forth the duties for public corporation audit committees as required by SEC rules and listing standards of major national securities exchanges:

- select and engage the corporation's external auditor; evaluate the auditor's independence, qualifications, and performance (including the engagement partner and other senior members of the audit staff); and determine, for each fiscal year, whether to continue that relationship or engage a different firm;
- review and approve annually the proposed terms of the external auditor's engagement, including the scope and plan of the audit and the fee arrangements;
- approve, before each engagement, any additional audit-related or non-audit services to be provided by the audit firm, based on the committee's judgment as to whether the firm is an appropriate choice to provide the additional services and whether the engagement might involve prohibited non-audit services or impair the firm's independence;
- set clear policies for hiring employees or former employees of the external auditors to avoid impairing the auditor's independence;
- serve as a channel of communication between the external auditor and the board and between the senior internal audit executive and the board;
- provide oversight of the internal audit function (NYSE-listed companies);
- oversee the corporation's compliance with legal and regulatory requirements;
- establish procedures to receive and respond to any complaints or concerns about the corporation's accounting, internal controls, or auditing matters, including procedures for the confidential and anonymous submission by employees of any such complaints or concerns;

- discuss with management the corporation's quarterly and annual earnings press releases, including consideration of the appropriateness and consistency of non-generally accepted accounting principles (GAAP) and other operating measures, and provide financial information and earnings guidance to analysts, the financial press, and rating agencies;
- review the corporation's annual and quarterly financial statements and management certifications, with both management and the external auditor, and discuss with each of them any major issues regarding accounting principles and financial statement presentation and the quality of management's accounting judgments in preparing the financial statements;
- review the "Management's Discussion and Analysis" section in each periodic report before filing it with the SEC, and discuss with management and the external auditor any questions or issues that arise in connection with that review;
- determine whether to recommend to the board that the audited annual financial statements be included in the corporation's annual report on SEC Form 10-K;
- review the effect of regulatory and accounting initiatives, as well as off-balance sheet arrangements, on the financial statements;
- consider, in consultation with the external auditor and the senior internal audit executive, if any, the adequacy and effectiveness of the corporation's internal controls, which, among other things, must be designed to provide reasonable assurance that the corporation's books and records are accurate, that its assets are safeguarded, and that the publicly reported financial statements prepared by management are presented fairly and in conformity with GAAP;
- review management's annual assessment of the effectiveness of the corporation's internal control over financial reporting and the external auditor's audit of internal control over financial reporting;
- receive and consider required communications from the external auditor as a result of its review of the quarterly financial statements;
- review with the external auditor any audit problems or difficulties, and management's response;

- review and approve the audit committee's annual report to shareholders required to be included in a public corporation's annual meeting proxy statement;
- discuss polices with respect to risk assessment and risk management; and
- report regularly to the board of directors on the committee's activities.

Other duties and responsibilities that many audit committees undertake as matters of good corporate practice include

- establish and oversee policies related to, and approve (in coordination with the corporation's nominating and governance committee) if appropriate, any related person transactions between the corporation and its officers or directors, or their family members or enterprises any of them control;
- establish a direct or "dotted-line" reporting relationship between the senior internal audit executive and the audit committee, with appropriate input in the hiring, compensation, performance review, and reassignment or termination of the senior internal audit executive, as well as approving internal audit plans and the budget for the internal audit group;
- consider the appropriate reporting relationship between the chief compliance officer and the audit committee;
- if provided, review the external auditor's management letter and management's responses to that letter (which generally includes comments on any control deficiencies observed during the audit and other recommendations arising from the audit);
- review SEC staff comments on filings;
- receive reports on significant matters considered by the corporation's disclosure committee, if any;
- meet privately with the corporation's legal counsel to review pending claims and litigation, possible loss contingencies, and other legal concerns, including procedures and policies for addressing legal and compliance issues and reduction of legal risk; for public companies, this generally occurs quarterly in connection with the review of the corporation's financial statements and SEC filings; and

- meet privately each quarter with the chief financial officer, chief accounting officer, chief compliance officer, and senior internal audit executive.

C. ENGAGING THE AUDITORS AND PRE-APPROVING THEIR SERVICES

One of the key roles of the audit committee is engaging and overseeing the corporation's external auditor. The audit committee reviews and approves the terms of engagement and compensation and should understand the scope of the audit. The audit committee must pre-approve all audit and non-audit services the external auditor performs during the year, as well as any audit-related services performed by any other auditing firm. The pre-approval process ensures that the audit committee will consider the effect of any audit and non-audit work on the auditor's independence. In addition, the external auditor must provide an annual letter about its independence to the audit committee of a public corporation. The committee must discuss this letter with the external auditor and consider what effect, if any, non-audit services that the auditor provides may have on the auditor's independence.

Many audit committees develop policies and procedures to pre-approve specific and detailed types of audit and non-audit services before the need for an engagement arises. Notably, the audit committee must pre-approve all tax services and internal control-related services engagement by engagement. Some committees delegate this pre-approval authority to the chair (or a subcommittee) of the audit committee to ensure that necessary services proceed efficiently, allowing for approval between audit committee meetings. Any individual or entity that has this authority must report all decisions to the full committee. The audit committee also reviews the hiring of any former personnel of the auditor to assure that it meets regulatory restrictions and will not affect the auditor's independence.

D. OVERSEEING THE INDEPENDENT AUDIT

The audit committee is responsible for evaluating annually the effectiveness of the external auditor, including reviewing the auditor's letter confirming its independence and discussing the firm's independence with the auditor, the auditor's knowledge of the financial issues and accounting standards of the industry or industries in which the corporation operates, and the timeliness and quality of the auditor's services. This evaluation should include discussing with the external auditor the results of the Public Company Accounting Oversight Board's annual evaluation of the audit firm.

The audit committee should meet with the external auditor during the planning phase of the annual audit to review the plan for the staffing, scope, and cost of the audit and to discuss any areas that may require emphasis or special procedures during the audit. The audit committee should review the auditor's opinion letter, including with respect to any critical audit matters identified in such opinion. After the audit, the committee should review with the external auditor any problems or difficulties encountered, any significant issues requiring discussion or debate with management during or after the audit, and any letter from the external auditor to management summarizing audit observations together with management's response to that letter.

The audit committee should understand significant accounting judgments and estimates that materially affect the corporation's financial statements. Corporations sometimes have a choice among available generally accepted accounting principles or practices. Therefore, the committee should inquire about and understand the effect of alternative choices on reported results. The audit committee should review, annually or as frequently as needed, with the external auditor and with the CFO or chief accounting officer, any significant issues regarding, and any changes in, choices of accounting principles. Some audit committees find it useful to ask the external auditor to inform the committee what choices the auditor would have made if it, rather than management, had been responsible for preparing the financial statements. The committee also must review with the auditor the quality of management's accounting judgments and estimates.

The audit committee should discuss, with the participation of the senior internal audit executive, any significant deficiencies or material weaknesses the external auditor identified during its annual audit of internal controls. If the external auditor identifies any significant deficiencies or material weaknesses in the corporation's internal control over financial reporting, the audit committee should oversee management's timely remediation of those deficiencies. If the audit committee fails to do so, the auditor may conclude that the audit committee itself constitutes a material weakness in the corporation's internal controls.

The above-discussed processes and reviews allow the audit committee to determine whether to recommend to the board inclusion of the audited financial statements in the corporation's annual report on SEC Form 10-K.

E. INTERACTION WITH INTERNAL AUDIT

The NYSE requires its listed companies to have an internal audit function. The internal auditors typically are employees of the corporation, but some corporations outsource some or all of this function to a firm that is not affiliated with its external auditor. The internal audit function should operate pursuant to a written charter approved by the committee.

The audit committee should routinely meet, in private, with the senior internal audit executive to discuss the relationship between the internal and external audit programs, to consider any problems or issues that may have occurred since the last meeting, and to review the implementation of any corrective actions recommended to management by internal audit. Before the fiscal year begins, the committee should approve the annual internal audit plan. The audit committee should ensure that the internal audit function has sufficient staff resources and budget to fulfill its internal audit plan for the coming year.

If the corporation does not have an internal audit function, the committee should consider with management and the external auditor whether to establish one and, if not, how to obtain the benefits and protections of such a function. If the corporation has outsourced the internal audit function, the committee should meet regularly with appropriate representatives of that service provider, including meeting in executive session.

F. MEETINGS WITH AUDITORS

Although the CFO or chief accounting officer normally attends meetings with external and internal auditors, the audit committee should also meet with the external and internal auditors in executive session, without management present. The NYSE requires the audit committees of listed companies to meet periodically with the external auditor and the senior internal audit executive separately, in executive session without the participation of other management. These sessions typically cover the following topics: whether (1) the auditors are uncomfortable with any matters regarding the corporation and its financial affairs and records, (2) the auditors have had any significant disagreements with management, (3) the auditors have had the full cooperation of management throughout the audit process, (4) the corporation has reasonably effective accounting systems and controls in place, and (5) the auditor recommends strengthening any material systems or controls or financial staffing. Many audit committees find it useful to have the external auditor describe the two or three areas that involved the most discussion with management during the course of the auditor's work. The committee may also meet with management to discuss the quality of services provided by the external and internal auditors.

The audit committee should discuss with the external auditor and management their respective roles with respect to the corporation's quarterly financial reports. They should also discuss the external auditor's procedure for raising with the committee or its chair significant deficiencies or material weaknesses in internal control over financial reporting and critical audit matters.

As part of the auditor's annual audit of the corporation's internal control over financial reporting, the external auditor must assess whether the audit committee understands and exercises its oversight responsibility over financial reporting and internal controls. As part of this assessment, the external auditor will consider the audit committee's knowledge about the corporation's accounting policies and internal controls and ability to monitor any control remediation efforts by management. If the auditor concludes that the audit committee's oversight is ineffective, the auditor must report that conclusion, in writing, to the board.

G. MEETING WITH COMPLIANCE OFFICERS

Unless there is another board committee responsible for compliance, the audit committee should meet as necessary and appropriate, typically on a quarterly basis, with the officers responsible for implementing the corporation's codes of business conduct and compliance policies. Officers with compliance responsibilities typically include the general counsel, senior internal audit executive, and chief compliance officer. These officers should meet with the audit committee in executive session outside the presence of other officers or directors who are not independent. The responsible officers should also report to the committee periodically. The scope and content of those reports should give the committee timely information about the number and type of concerns reported and investigated, any material violations of law or corporate policies, the disciplinary actions taken, and any other information to enable the committee to monitor the effectiveness of the overall compliance program. These officers also should report annually on how the elements of the compliance program satisfy applicable legal requirements. In addition, the general counsel should meet regularly with the audit committee, or another committee of independent directors, to communicate concerns regarding litigation and legal compliance matters, including potential or ongoing material violations of law by the corporation and breaches by senior managers of fiduciary duties, violation of corporate policies, or ethical violations.

H. ESTABLISHING PROCEDURES TO HANDLE COMPLAINTS

The audit committee of a public corporation must establish procedures for employees to report anonymously and confidentially concerns or complaints about accounting, internal controls, and auditing matters, as well as violations of the corporation's code of ethics. For global companies, the procedures must comply with the privacy regimes of multiple countries. Audit committee members are not usually in the best position to conduct fact-finding or even to receive complaints or concerns in the first instance. Instead, the committee should create, with management's assistance, procedures adequate to ensure that information reaches the committee in a form conducive to identifying "red flags" and to ensuring timely and efficient review and resolution of any issues. For example, the audit committee may decide to rely on an ethics or compliance officer to gather, review, and process information, or it may decide to outsource this task to a third-party service provider.

In addition, lawyers for public companies (both internal and outside counsel) may be required by law to report to a committee of independent directors, or to the board, credible evidence that a material violation of securities laws, breach of fiduciary duty, or similar violation by the issuer or any of its officers, directors, employees, or agents has occurred, is occurring, or is about to occur. Public companies may determine that the audit committee is the appropriate committee to receive these reports. If so, the audit committee should have an effective process for acting on reports, including an understanding about arranging for legal advice from outside counsel when appropriate.

I. MEETINGS, TIME COMMITMENT, AND COMPENSATION

The audit committee should discuss and determine the number of meetings it needs to hold to deal effectively with its responsibilities. The listing standards of major national securities exchanges require audit committees to review quarterly and annual reports filed with the SEC. It is common for public corporation audit committees to have an in-person or telephonic meeting with the corporation's CEO, CFO, other senior financial managers, and external auditor in advance of each quarterly earnings release. As a result, almost all audit committees schedule at least four, and some as many as five to eight, meetings per year.

It is important that the schedule for board and other committee meetings and activities not unduly limit the time for audit committee deliberations. Membership on the audit committee requires a significant commitment of time. Committee meetings are often several hours in length, and some extend for an entire day. As a result, some boards provide the audit committee members with a higher level of compensation, often through an additional retainer for committee service. Others have determined that differential compensation among board committee members can create the risk of divisions within the board and may make selection of members and rotation of committee assignments more difficult.

CHAPTER

8 Compensation Committee

Executive compensation plays a central role in attracting, retaining, and motivating the management talent critical to the corporation's success. The compensation committee is responsible for designing and approving executive compensation and may perform other responsibilities as discussed in this chapter. The integrity and transparency of the committee's decision-making process are of paramount concern to shareholders and regulators. To fulfill their fiduciary duties, directors involved in the process must act in good faith and on an informed basis. Abuses and perceived excesses in executive compensation policies, plans, and programs combined with investors' desire for greater transparency lead to many federal disclosure and corporate governance reforms related to executive compensation.

These changes include rules requiring mandatory say-on-pay votes for all public companies and executive compensation disclosures relating to the relationship between the CEO's total pay and the corporation's median employees' total pay as well as the relationship between executive compensation and the corporation's financial performance.

These reforms have resulted in a clear focus on the role of the compensation committee as the primary corporate decision maker for compensation matters. In performing this function, the public corporation compensation committee should consider the following questions:

- How are compensation packages for the CEO and other senior executives determined, including (1) who negotiates the arrangements, (2) what are the relevant peer companies with which to compare the corporation's compensation packages, and (3) what is the appropriate role, if any, for compensation consultants and other advisors in designing the compensation program elements and setting compensation levels?

- Is management's compensation reasonably related to personal and corporate performance?
- Does it appropriately motivate management to achieve strategic objectives and build value for shareholders while encouraging legal compliance and behaviors in line with desired corporate culture?
- Over time, are the compensation programs and policies attracting and retaining quality management talent for the corporation?
- Do a corporation's public disclosures about executive compensation give shareholders, proxy advisory firms, and other stakeholders an accurate picture of senior executive compensation and the reasoning behind executive compensation decisions?
- Under what circumstances should the corporation recover previously awarded compensation, and how should the corporation's compensation "clawback" policy function, given legislative and regulatory requirements, including (1) which officers and employees will be subject to the policy, (2) what types and amounts of compensation are subject to potential recovery, and (3) how will the policy be implemented to ensure enforceability?
- Are severance, change-of-control, and post-employment benefits appropriately correlated to corporate interests and reasonable in amount?

The compensation committee should apply independent judgment to determine an overarching compensation philosophy for the corporation and the components of the compensation arrangements, as well as the levels that are in the best interests of the corporation. When functioning effectively, the compensation committee provides credibility and substance to the concept of independent oversight of executive compensation.

A. MEMBERSHIP

For public companies, the compensation committee must consist solely of independent directors. The listing standards of major national securities exchanges require that compensation committee members satisfy independence standards that are more stringent than those applicable to directors generally. Moreover, SEC rules exempt executive officer equity grants from short-swing profit recapture only if "non-employee directors," as defined in those rules, make the grant decisions. This term is similar to, but not the same as, the "independent director" definitions in major national securities exchange listing standards. Consequently, the eligibility of prospective compensation committee members should be reviewed against each standard. Interlocking compensation committee memberships are undesirable because they trigger additional proxy statement disclosures and may disqualify a director from independent status under listing standards. For example, if an executive officer of a corporation serves on the compensation committee of another corporation, and an executive officer of that other corporation serves on the first corporation's compensation committee, they are interlocking.

Apart from legal considerations, the compensation committee's independence from management gives credibility to how the compensation committee exercises its key responsibility: to establish and approve compensation for executive officers on behalf of the corporation. Even when a director meets the independence requirements of the applicable SEC rules and listing standards of major national securities exchanges, close personal or business ties between the director and the CEO may mean, or at least create the appearance of, conflicts of interest that would indicate the director is not an appropriate member of the compensation committee.

B. PRINCIPAL FUNCTIONS

The principal functions of a public corporation compensation committee are to

- oversee the corporation's overall compensation structure, philosophy, policies, and programs and assess whether they establish appropriate incentives for senior executives;
- review and approve goals and objectives established for CEO and senior executive compensation that align with board-approved corporate goals and objectives and annually evaluate executive performance in light of those goals and objectives;
- establish or make a recommendation to the independent directors of the board about the compensation and benefits of the CEO and certain senior executive officers;
- assess how compensation policies and programs contribute to or affect the corporation's risk profile and structure them to

create incentives for management to make risk-appropriate decisions;
- evaluate and approve employment agreements with executive officers;
- establish and periodically review policies for the administration of executive compensation programs (including all equity-based plans and perquisites);
- make recommendations to the board with respect to incentive compensation plans and equity-based plans generally;
- consider the results of advisory say-on-pay votes;
- review and understand applicable policies and voting recommendations of proxy advisory firms that carry significant influence with institutional shareholders;
- review and concur in the corporation's Compensation Discussion and Analysis (CD&A) disclosure in the corporation's annual meeting proxy statement or annual report on Form 10-K and discuss with management any issues or questions; and
- review and approve, if required, the annual report of the compensation committee for inclusion in the annual meeting proxy statement or annual report on Form 10-K.

1. Decision-Making Process

The compensation committee independence requirement is designed to promote objective judgment on the sensitive matter of management's compensation and, in particular, the compensation of the CEO. The compensation committee should consider the most effective process for reaching an independent and informed decision about the appropriateness of the amount and composition of the CEO's and executive management's compensation packages.

Management's participation in the compensation committee's decision-making process is a particularly sensitive area. Both the reality and the appearance of independent oversight are important. It is wise to have a process in place that facilitates substantive executive sessions for committee discussions on executive compensation matters that occur without members of management present. Although a CEO will review his or her performance and the performance of the senior executive team, a member of management should never be present during deliberations regarding his or her own compensation. The committee should consider the CEO's compensation in a private session, without the CEO or the CEO's subordinate officers. Independent compensation consultants or counsel typically are present throughout the compensation committee meeting, including during these executive sessions in the compensation committee's discretion.

2. Independent Advice

The compensation committee may benefit from the advice of independent compensation consultants or counsel who can assist in collecting comparative data and advise on the compensation packages best suited to achieving the corporation's long-term strategic objectives. The listing standards of major national securities exchanges require that committees have the power to hire (without management influence in the selection process) compensation specialists, consulting firms, or other experts. These outside advisors may assist in the evaluation of executive officers and the development of a compensation program so that the committee need not rely solely on corporate personnel or management-selected outside specialists for advice and guidance. State corporate law protects directors in relying in good faith on information, opinions, and reports by experts selected with reasonable care.

Given the importance of executive compensation and corporate governance at public companies, the committee should consider the following factors before engaging an advisor: (1) other services performed by the advisor for the corporation, (2) fees paid to the advisor for those services, and (3) existing personal and business relationships between the advisor and the corporation, including those with management. At all times following the engagement, the compensation committee should be aware of any new relationships that develop between the advisor and the corporation or management.

The compensation committee's need for independent advice is particularly critical when the compensation committee exercises its obligations with respect to reviewing and approving employment, retention, change-in-control, and severance agreements with executives. Listing standards of major national securities exchanges give compensation committees authority to approve their advisors' fees and other terms of engagement making it clear that the advisors work for the compensation committee, not management. The advisor should have direct access to the compensation committee, without management present, to help preserve the advisor's independence. Outside advisors should also have direct access to senior executives in order to obtain information necessary to provide the compensation committee with independent advice. Compensation consultant fees and other consultant services must be publicly disclosed in certain circumstances.

Regardless of whether the committee engages outside compensation consultants or counsel for assistance, the committee is ultimately responsible for approving the terms, amounts, and forms of compensation and cannot substitute the advice of advisors for its own business judgment.

3. Structure and Components of Executive Compensation

The basic principle that a significant portion of an executive's compensation should be tied to the corporation's strategic objectives and financial performance, with an appropriate balance between short- and long-term incentives, should guide the compensation committee. The structure and components of an executive compensation package vary among industries and companies. Benchmarking against peer companies is sometimes used as a tool when setting or reviewing executive compensation, but the committee should avoid simply matching the design or amounts of compensation at peer companies and be mindful of differentiating factors such as the corporation's culture and values and desired behaviors. Peer companies should be selected carefully and reviewed regularly, with corporation size, financial condition, industry characteristics, competitive factors, risk profile, and location as relevant factors. Some companies have compensation consultants prepare summaries focused on the regions in which the companies compete for talent, the industries in which they are engaged, and their market capitalization. If the markets for which the companies compete for executive talent differ for one or more positions, some companies use more than one peer group for executives.

Compensation committees have a wide variety of tools for equity incentives, such as restricted stock, restricted stock units, stock appreciation rights, stock options, and other types of equity compensation. Although at one time options were the favored vehicle for equity pay, more recently corporations have included other forms of equity compensation, such as restricted stock or restricted stock units, sometimes with extended vesting or vesting based on specified performance goals. In choosing the form, vesting schedule, and conditions of an award, compensation committees should consider whether the award provides the intended incentive, for example, by considering other awards already held, including the exercise prices and vesting schedule of those awards.

When granting awards, the compensation committee should be informed about and understand the accounting treatment of the awards, the tax effect of the awards for both the corporation and the individual, and the administrative complexity of the awards. The compensation committee members should also be informed about and understand the calculation and achievement of any financial performance metrics and targets. Likewise, the audit committee should understand financial statement implications of executive compensation programs. As a result, compensation committees often request audit committee review of the calculations for financial performance metrics prior to compensation committee review and approval of any annual cash or equity incentive compensation awards. For these reasons, boards may choose to have some overlapping membership between the audit and compensation committees.

Compensation committees also often require retention or holding periods for stock, whether obtained on option exercise or as restricted stock. Retention policies can help align an executive's economic interest more effectively with long-term corporation performance. Some companies also establish stock ownership targets to further align the executives' interests with those of shareholders. Most companies prohibit activities that attempt to hedge against a decrease in the value of the corporation's equity securities. The SEC requires that public companies disclose policies governing whether employees or directors may engage in hedging transactions.

The compensation committee should also review the benefits and perquisites (often called perks) provided to senior executives, particularly when approving employment contracts. Perks have received considerable attention due to perceived excesses in their use, such as personal use of corporate aircraft, tax gross-ups, and use of corporation resources post-employment. The SEC requires disclosure of perks that in aggregate exceed $10,000 in value annually and has brought enforcement actions against corporations for failing to disclose perks as required. Other important areas of scrutiny are retirement, termination, and change-in-control benefits. There is widespread shareholder concern that these benefits are not sufficiently related to job performance, and compensation committees should be aware that these benefits could be viewed as excessive even when fully disclosed. For example, proxy advisory firms often recommend that constituents withhold votes from or vote against directors who are members of the compensation committee of a board of directors that has approved a new or materially modified employment agreement that includes a tax gross-up.

In addition, committee members should understand the interplay of all compensation arrangements—fixed, incentive, benefits, perks, deferred compensation, retirement, severance, and change in control—so that unintended or disproportionate benefits do not accrue to the senior executive. To facilitate this understanding, at many public corporations, management or independent compensation consultants annually provide committee members with a clear and comprehensive presentation detailing all elements and amounts of compensation paid to each senior executive, as well as the value of potential retirement, severance, and change-in-control benefits to which the executive could become entitled (sometimes referred to as a tally sheet). The SEC's rules require public corporations to disclose details about the dollar value of all elements of executive compensation, as well as estimates of benefits that could become payable to senior executives either upon a termination of employment or upon a change in control of the corporation.

The compensation committee also has a role in risk oversight for public corporation compensation policies and practices. Under SEC rules, public companies must analyze their compensation policies and practices and disclose whether those policies and practices encourage excessive risk taking and are reasonably likely to have a material adverse effect on the corporation. In most corporations, management, in some cases working with compensation consultants, prepares this analysis and makes the initial determination regarding the companies' policies and practices by tallying all elements of compensation, determining the risks posed by each element, and then analyzing any mitigating factors. The compensation committee, however, retains an oversight role, and management should detail its procedures for committee approval and provide the committee with a summary of its analysis and determination. In some cases, the compensation committee may want to review and approve management's comprehensive analysis or even conduct its own analysis with input from its compensation consultants.

The proper design of a compensation program is just the starting point. The program should require at least annual performance evaluations of the participating executives against pre-established performance targets (which may include comparison against the performance of peer corporations), as well as ongoing review of the program's effectiveness. The compensation committee should keep the board informed of the results of these periodic reviews.

4. Documentation of Approval of Executive Compensation

The compensation committee should review with senior management the corporation's procedures for accurately and timely documenting the grants or issuances of equity awards, both in the compensation committee's minutes (or other written action) and in the documentation evidencing the awards. Compensation committee minutes or resolutions that adequately discuss the compensation committee's rationale, deliberation, and consideration regarding the grants or issuances of equity awards and any other form of executive compensation are considered good practice and can assist the corporation in preparing, if required, its annual CD&A in its proxy statement. As a general matter, a corporation should have adequate written procedures relating to the grant or issuance of equity awards, including timing and pricing, to help protect the corporation, its executives, and the compensation committee against claims of manipulation or abuse. Good practices also include granting equity awards pursuant to a program, plan, or practice, such as at pre-scheduled meetings or on a pre-determined date. These practices can mitigate against potential timing issues related to the release of non-public information or that fall outside of corporation blackout periods for employee trading of corporation securities. Although the use of written consents and delegations of authority involving grants of equity compensation to non-Section 16 officers is not uncommon, the use of such mechanisms for CEO and executive officer compensation actions is not advisable because it may suggest insufficient process or deliberation sufficient to meet the directors' fiduciary duties.

5. Legal Restrictions on Executive Compensation

The compensation committee should become familiar with and receive legal advice about legal restrictions on compensation to officers and directors. Federal securities law prohibits most personal loans and extensions or arrangements of credit from a public corporation to its directors and executive officers. In addition, under federal securities law, the SEC has sought, and may continue to seek, recoupment of bonuses, incentive- or equity-based compensation, and profits from the sale of securities from CEOs and CFOs following accounting restatements of their companies involving financial misconduct. It is also possible there could be new SEC regulations or listing standards of major national securities exchanges regarding clawbacks of executive compensation after financial or other misdeeds.

Regardless of the requirements of the federal securities and other laws, in circumstances in which there has been a restatement indicating that the bases on which incentive-based compensation has been paid are no longer correct, the compensation committee or other independent directors should consider whether to recover any compensation under the state law doctrine of unjust enrichment. In addition, if the restatement resulted from employee misconduct, the compensation committee or other independent directors should consider whether to take action to discipline or dismiss, as well as to recover compensation paid to, any employee involved in the misconduct.

To assist with the recovery of such compensation, the compensation committee should incorporate clawback provisions into the terms of incentive compensation programs or arrangements. In particular, the compensation committee should determine the circumstances under which the corporation would be entitled to clawback. Such circumstances should include determining the covered employees and types and amounts of compensation to be subject to the policy, as well as determining how to implement the policy, taking into consideration the corporation's ability to enforce the provision under relevant law.

C. DISCLOSURE OF COMPENSATION DECISIONS

The annual meeting proxy statement for larger public companies must include a CD&A, which is a detailed discussion of the key elements of the corporation's executive compensation policies and decisions. This disclosure discusses the principles underlying executive compensation decisions and should explain the rationale behind the adoption of those principles and the executive compensation decisions in light of the principles.

The CD&A must include a discussion of the following:

- the philosophy and objectives of the corporation's compensation programs;
- the results the compensation program is designed to reward;
- the elements of compensation;
- the reasons the corporation chose to pay each element, including any adjustments;
- the way the corporation determines the amount (and the formula, if any) for each element of pay; and
- the way each compensation element and the corporation's decisions regarding that element fit into the corporation's overall compensation objectives and affect decisions regarding other compensation elements.

Consultation with external compensation specialists may be necessary to assist the committee in formulating the CD&A. Because the committee makes decisions for senior executives outside the presence of management, the committee should assist management in its preparation of the CD&A by reviewing the disclosure to confirm it reflects and highlights the various factors the compensation committee weighed and considered. After the compensation committee's review and discussion of the CD&A, it should be satisfied with the disclosure's accuracy. The compensation committee must also state, in a separate report in the proxy statement, that its members have reviewed and discussed the CD&A with management and, based on this review and discussion, recommended that it be included in the proxy statement.

The compensation committee should seek appropriate assurances from management and legal counsel that all disclosures required by law and by the applicable national securities exchange listing standards are being made, and that rules related to shareholder approval of equity compensation plans and the reporting of grants of and trades in the corporation's securities are being observed. The compensation committee, along with counsel, should discuss and consider how to document adequately the process leading to the compensation disclosures in a manner that supports the disclosures made.

Public companies must hold a non-binding shareholder vote, at least once every three years, to approve compensation of the executive officers named in the proxy statement. Corporations must also hold a non-binding vote every six years to determine the frequency of say-on-pay votes.

In addition, SEC rules require corporations, depending on their SEC filing status, to make specific disclosures, including

- indicating whether the committee retained a consultant and its consideration of the factors for doing so;
- indicating whether the committee's work has raised any conflicts of interest, and if so, how they were resolved;
- demonstrating the relationship between executive compensation and financial performance;
- stating the ratio between the CEO's compensation and the median compensation of all other employees; and
- indicating whether certain hedging transactions are permitted.

D. DIRECTOR COMPENSATION

Decisions about director compensation reside with the board. Usually, it is more efficient for the board to delegate director compensation to either the compensation committee or the nominating and governance committee, both of which would ultimately make a recommendation on a director compensation program to the board for its review and approval. Many boards find it is more efficient for the compensation committee to handle this responsibility because it is better versed in the relevant subject matter, including understanding the design of compensation programs, financial and tax impacts, and reporting and disclosure obligations. Other boards may find that the nominating and governance committee is appropriate because of its core responsibilities for director and board matters, familiarity with the compensation implications of director recruitment, and understanding of the director skills and qualifications relevant to establishing the director pay peer group, as well as its structural separation from executive compensation matters.

The director compensation program should be carefully and fairly designed to ensure the corporation is positioned to attract and retain the best-qualified individuals by fairly compensating its directors, while guarding against the potential for claims or challenges that such compensation is excessive or impairs non-management director independence. The appropriate board committee periodically evaluates the form and amount of director compensation and makes recommendations to the board about whether to modify the corporation's director compensation program. The committee typically seeks the advice of an independent compensation consultant. Directors have an unavoidable conflict of interest in fixing their own compensation, and they cannot eliminate the conflict by having management or an independent compensation consultant suggest the director compensation programs. Directors nevertheless have the responsibility to determine their own compensation, so they must ensure they engage in a thorough, deliberative decision-making process and can demonstrate they have considered the information or received independent advice necessary to reach a fair decision. That process should include data on peer companies and relevant market practices, as well as an analysis of any factors relating to their particular circumstance, such as the complexity of the corporation and a director's expected time commitment. In setting their own compensation, directors should be mindful that doing so is an interested transaction subject to heightened judicial review if challenged, and therefore they should take extra care in the approach and be able to justify the decision made. In some circumstances, seeking stockholder approval or ratification of director compensation may be appropriate to protect the action.

To maintain directors' focus on appropriate long-range corporate objectives, most corporations grant full-value awards in the form of restricted stock grants or restricted stock units. Many corporations have stock ownership guidelines requiring directors to hold a minimum amount of corporation stock while serving as a director.

Directors generally are given a period following initial appointment to meet the stock ownership requirement. In addition, some corporations have included annual limits on director compensation as part of their shareholder-approved equity incentive plan.

Director compensation programs should align the directors' interests with the long-term interests of the corporation. Director compensation may take several different forms, including annual stock or cash retainers, attendance fees for board and committee meetings, deferred compensation plans, stock options, restricted stock units, and restricted stock grants. Additional compensation for additional service, such as for serving as independent board chair, lead independent director, chair of a committee, member of a special committee, or membership on a particularly active committee, is also possible. The corporation's executives generally do not receive additional compensation for board service.

SEC proxy disclosure rules require detailed disclosure of all elements of director compensation and the processes for determining director compensation, including any perquisites and charitable donation programs. Any consulting or other agreements with directors and any payments to directors for consulting or other services beyond the regular directors' compensation program can impair independence and require disclosure in the annual proxy statement. The board should be sensitive to and avoid compensation policies or corporate perquisites that might impair the independence of its non-management directors.

E. ADDITIONAL RESPONSIBILITIES
1. Areas of Expanded Committee Scope

Compensation committees focus their time in areas beyond designing and approving executive compensation programs and related responsibilities. These areas generally reflect the significance of human resources, and compensation committee engagement with the chief human resources officer, to the corporation's overall strategy, operations, performance, and risk profile. These responsibilities may be delegated by the board to the compensation committee through the committee's charter or may be topics or activities taken up by the compensation committee at the direction of the board or the chair of the compensation committee. These areas may include

- succession planning for the CEO and executive management (if not addressed by the nominating and governance committee as discussed in Chapter 9);

- oversight of leadership and talent development programs;
- engagement with internal successors or high potential talent;
- diversity and inclusion;
- pay equity;
- workplace conduct issues such as sexual harassment;
- corporate culture and employee engagement;
- oversight of risks associated with human capital management and workforce planning; and
- reviewing and monitoring the effectiveness of general employee compensation plans, employee pension, profit sharing, 401(k), and other benefit plans and employee programs.

Compensation committees that take on broader responsibilities may want to consider expanding the name of the committee to reflect the expanded scope.

2. ERISA Fiduciary Considerations

Compensation committees should consider whether they are or should be fiduciaries with respect to the corporation's pension, 401(k), or other employee benefit plans that are subject to regulation under the Employee Retirement Income Security Act (ERISA). Under ERISA, plan fiduciaries are subject to heightened scrutiny and responsibility with respect to the investment of plan assets. The compensation committee has a duty to be informed about the corporation's compensation and benefit structure; but most compensation committees do not act as fiduciaries for ERISA-covered benefit plans. Directors and high-level executives typically are privy to non-public information regarding the corporation's performance and finances. As a result, they can be in the difficult position of having to choose between their duties as officers or directors under state and federal laws to keep such information confidential and their duties as plan fiduciaries to disclose or act upon such information for the benefit of plan participants. Generally, rather than having directors or senior officers designated as plan fiduciaries, corporation employees (but not the most-senior executives) and/or independent third parties will serve as the fiduciaries of the corporation's ERISA-covered benefit plans. If the board or compensation committee delegates ERISA fiduciary duties to qualified appointees, those appointments must be made prudently and in the best interests of plan participants as required by ERISA. The compensation committee or board should still exercise some oversight, usually through periodic reports on the plans being administered, in order to satisfy themselves that the appointees are fulfilling their delegated duties.

CHAPTER 9

Nominating and Governance Committee

An effective nominating and corporate governance committee is critical to board performance. This committee's stature and importance are tied to the fact that a corporation's investors are often focused on the quality and strength of a corporation's board and governance systems.

Major national securities exchange listing standards prescribe some elements of the nominating and corporate governance function. Generally, the committee is responsible for recruiting and maintaining board members with the appropriate skills and independence for quality decision making. It also implements and oversees the operation of corporate governance principles for both board process and the corporation's business.

A. MEMBERSHIP

The nominating and governance committee should be composed solely of independent directors. The NYSE requires that each of its listed companies has a nominating and governance committee composed entirely of independent directors, with a written charter that addresses the committee's purposes and responsibilities, which include identifying individuals qualified to become directors; selecting, or recommending that the board select, director nominees; developing and recommending to the board a set of corporate governance principles for the corporation; and overseeing the evaluation of the board and management. Listing standards for the Nasdaq Market do not mandate a nominating or corporate governance committee but do require that either a committee of independent directors (subject to limited exceptions) or a majority of independent board members select or recommend director nominees.

B. CRITERIA FOR BOARD MEMBERSHIP

A nominating and governance committee should establish, or recommend to the board, criteria for identifying appropriate director candidates. These criteria are usually set forth in corporate governance principles or a separate policy. The committee should lead the recruitment and selection process. The attributes of an effective corporate director include strength of character, an inquiring and independent mind, practical wisdom, and mature judgment. In addition to these personal qualities, the committee may want to emphasize individual qualifications, such as technical skills, career specialization, specific industry experience, or expertise in matters such as finance, compensation, or governance. Other important areas of expertise may change over time and may depend on a corporation's specific needs. They may include, for example, expertise in regulatory matters, risk management, cybersecurity, and global management. The effective nominating and governance committee seeks director attributes to complement and expand the attributes of the existing board members. The committee must identify a director who qualifies as an "audit committee financial expert" for accounting and financial reporting purposes, or the corporation must explain in its annual proxy statement why the committee does not have such an expert. There is also an emphasis on diversity, recognizing that diversity can contribute significant value by providing additional perspectives to board deliberations. The articles or certificate of incorporation, bylaws, or board policies may include other qualifications for directors, such as age, length of service limitations, or relevant experience.

There is no one-size-fits-all approach to director searches. The desired outcome is a board with diverse experience relevant to the corporation's business that can build consensus and effectively exercise collaborative judgment and, when appropriate, challenge management. Board refreshment processes such as performing rigorous evaluations of the board and individual directors can inform the attributes sought in director searches. Some boards look for specific skills and experiences to build on what they currently possess, lack, or need to strengthen. This type of focus can help direct the search toward candidates who can provide needed additional talent and experience to the corporation.

Many corporate governance commentators recommend that a public corporation board have a substantial majority of independent directors, and the major national securities exchanges require at least a majority of directors who are independent as measured against the independence definition of the applicable exchange. When considering director independence, the committee should also bear in mind broader judicial standards of disinterestedness applicable for judicial review of conflict of interest or other issues. As a result, the committee should evaluate the full range of business and personal relationships between director candidates and the corporation and its senior managers in assessing a candidate's independence.

The board must be able to receive candid input from senior management. In addition to input from the CEO, who is typically on the board, the committee should consider how best to access senior management to ensure that input. Some nominating and governance committees determine that certain senior officers, in addition to the CEO, should serve as directors. Others decide that attendance at board or committee meetings by senior officers in a non-director capacity is sufficient to facilitate the board's ready access to information regarding the business and operations of the corporation. Although it is not typical, the presence of senior executives beyond the CEO on the board can serve to enhance, through firsthand contact, succession planning and facilitate peer relationships.

C. EVALUATING BOARD INCUMBENTS

The nominating and governance committee is usually responsible for developing and overseeing the processes for evaluating the board, its committees, and incumbent directors. Tools to assist in the evaluation process may include board, committee, or individual self-evaluations; peer evaluations; and confidential discussions led by the chair, lead independent director, or nominating and governance committee chair. Outside consultants can also be effective in administering the evaluation process. The feedback and results gathered from these and other governance processes serve to support the committee's deliberation and consideration of each director's contribution and the needs of the board before deciding whether to recommend renomination of an incumbent director. This practice can help address the common criticism that election or appointment to the board is tantamount to tenure. It is also responsive to SEC disclosure rules requiring disclosure of director qualifications relevant to serving on the corporation's board. Conducting board and committee evaluations annually helps to ensure effective performance and oversight. In addition to evaluating board structures and processes, the committee should assess the contributions and performance of individual directors based on their attendance, preparation, participation, and other relevant factors.

Boards handle the sensitive issue of board succession, including underperforming directors, in a variety of ways. Some boards attempt to deal with the issue indirectly through the adoption of mandatory retirement policies or limits on tenure, but these policies can create an expectation that board service continues until retirement or the term limit. In fact, a well-functioning nominating and governance committee should be able to decline to nominate incumbents for reelection as individual situations dictate.

D. NOMINATING DIRECTORS

The nominating and governance committee approves and selects, or recommends that the board select, director nominees, including both incumbent directors and new candidates. The committee also recommends candidates to the board to fill interim director vacancies or the addition of new directors between annual meetings.

The committee should encourage all directors, including management directors, to suggest candidates for the board. The committee should also seek out candidates and can employ search consultants to assist in identifying appropriate candidates. The committee's charter should give the committee the authority to retain a search firm to identify director candidates, including the authority to approve the search firm's fees and other retention terms. The committee should control the process, including making decisions with respect to nominees and recommending to the board a slate of nominees. Moreover, the committee should be the conduit for communication regarding shareholder recommendations for director nominees. The board's comprehensive plan for shareholder communications may encourage the committee to seek suggestions for director candidates from its institutional investors and other shareholders. Both the independent chair, if there is one, or a lead independent director and the nominating and governance committee chair should be prominently involved in the recruiting process to ensure that the committee is making the nominating decisions and not the CEO or other insiders.

Public corporation proxy statements must disclose the nominating and governance committee's procedures and policies for considering director candidates, as well as the particular experience, attributes, skills, and qualifications the committee focused on in selecting or recommending each director candidate. In addition to a summary of this information, some companies disclose a board skills matrix that indicates how each member contributes specific qualifications, attributes, skills, and experience to the board. Also, companies often disclose individual profiles of each director, including biographical data, a summary of the individual's professional experience, and an explanation of his or her relevant qualifications, attributes, skills, and experience. The proxy statement affords a board the opportunity to explain why it believes a nomination is warranted.

Furthermore, public companies must disclose whether, and if so how, the nominating and governance committee considers diversity in identifying director nominees. If the nominating and governance committee has a diversity policy, the corporation must disclose how the policy is applied and how the committee assesses the policy's effectiveness. The purpose of these disclosure requirements is to increase shareholder understanding of the nominating process. Accordingly, the committee should review its procedures and policies to ensure that they are consistent with the committee's circumstances and operations and that they are sufficiently formalized to provide clarity and to satisfy the scrutiny of public disclosure.

E. RECOMMENDING COMMITTEE MEMBERS AND CHAIRS

The nominating and governance committee also makes recommendations to the board about the responsibilities and organization of all board committees. The committee should recommend qualifications for membership on committees. The committee may also make annual recommendations of specific individuals for membership on and leadership of committees. Some boards have a policy of periodic rotation of committee memberships among the directors to develop expertise and allocate equitably the time commitment. The nominating and governance committee usually oversees this process.

F. CHIEF EXECUTIVE OFFICER AND OTHER MANAGEMENT SUCCESSION

One of the most important functions of the board is selecting and assessing the CEO and planning for the succession of the CEO and other executive officers. Ongoing planning for what happens in the event of a vacancy in leadership is a critical board responsibility. Boards may look to the nominating and governance committee to support or lead this process, particularly in an emergency situation.

The choice of a new CEO is fundamental to the direction of the corporation. The CEO is primarily responsible for implementing the corporation's strategic vision with input and guidance from the board. The CEO is also responsible for the short- and long-term performance of the corporation. He or he establishes the "tone at the top" for legal compliance and ethical standards. Finally, the CEO is generally responsible for the selection and direction of other members of senior management. Consequently, the board must select and continually assess the CEO with care and due consideration for the challenges facing the corporation. The board must monitor the CEO's performance and determine when there is a need for a change in senior management in light of executive performance and the corporation's challenges.

The nominating and governance committee often has the responsibility to recommend to the board a selection process for a successor to the CEO in the event of retirement, termination of service, or other reason for a vacancy. The committee may also review and approve proposed changes in other senior management positions, with the understanding that the CEO should have considerable discretion in selecting, retaining, and reviewing members of the management team. To perform these functions, the committee, or another board committee should, at least annually, review the performance of the CEO and members of senior management.

Succession planning is a continuous board activity that is closely related to management development. The board should be aware of, and regularly reassess, how long the current CEO is likely to continue, and what developments may cause a change in that expectation (including a shift in strategy, a change in performance, or an emergency or crisis). The board should also consider what might cause the CEO or other senior executive officers to contemplate leaving the corporation. Succession planning rarely results in a hard and fast plan for a specific outcome. Two key components of succession planning are assessing and developing other management talent and considering what steps the CEO and other senior executive officers can take to further develop their own leadership capabilities and those of their direct reports.

Decisions about succession planning and management development should be coordinated with corporate strategy because the leadership group must have both an understanding of the corporate strategy and the ability to implement it. In addition, the committee should ensure the succession plan includes emergency procedures for management succession in the event of the unexpected death, disability, or departure of the CEO. The plan should also incorporate a review, with the CEO, of management's plans for the replacement of members of the senior management team, as well as the CEO's assessment of the ability of team members to lead, whether on an interim or longer basis, should the CEO be incapacitated.

G. OTHER COMMITTEE AND CORPORATE GOVERNANCE FUNCTIONS

The nominating and governance committee typically is responsible for ensuring that the corporation has adopted, maintains, and regularly updates principles and policies of corporate governance. In addition to addressing director nomination or renomination and committee membership, the committee typically addresses the following tasks and issues:

- developing, recommending to the board, and monitoring a statement of corporate governance principles or guidelines (required of listed companies by NYSE);
- developing proposals for amendments to bylaws, certificates or articles of incorporation, board committee charters, and other governance documents or board-level policies;
- developing policies to respond to shareholder proposals;
- evaluating the effectiveness of individual directors, the board, and board committees (also required by NYSE);
- evaluating director standards of independence and monitoring director compliance with those standards;
- providing for director orientation and education programs;
- reviewing the board's leadership structure;
- reviewing the board committee structure, including each committee's recommendation regarding its charter and size, as well as the possible addition of other committees, such as finance, public policy, or risk management committees;
- reviewing and making recommendations with respect to the corporation's director policies, such as director compensation (if not addressed by the compensation committee; see Chapter 8 for a discussion on director compensation), retirement, indemnification, and insurance;
- reviewing and making recommendations with respect to the corporation's code of business conduct and ethics;
- monitoring and reviewing related party transactions or conflicts of interest;
- examining board meeting policies, such as meeting schedule and location, meeting agenda, presence and participation of non-director senior executives, and materials distributed in advance of meetings;

- establishing and disclosing the corporation's policy and procedures for shareholder communications with directors; and
- overseeing the corporation's program for shareholder engagement.

H. BOARD LEADERSHIP

As discussed in Chapter 5, many companies that do not have an independent non-executive board chair often designate an independent director as a presiding, lead, or other director designation indicating a leadership role among independent directors. This director can be a helpful counterweight to and business partner of a strong CEO. Importantly, the presiding or lead independent director can ensure that there is an appropriate flow of information to all board members. The nominating and governance committee should consider the appropriateness of such a designation. If it concludes that it should propose a candidate for the board's consideration, it should do so, along with a description of responsibilities. In many cases, the chair of the nominating and governance committee may be the appropriate person for this leadership role. Federal securities laws and regulations require companies to disclose their board leadership structure and the rationale for it.

CHAPTER 10

The Relationship between the Board of Directors and Shareholders

Under state law, responsibility for managing the business and affairs of the corporation is vested in the board of directors. Shareholders do not have direct management rights or responsibilities under state law. Instead, shareholders influence the corporation principally by voting in director elections and on certain other fundamental matters. Shareholders also have the right under U.S. securities laws to cast advisory votes on executive compensation and to request votes on other corporate governance and policy matters. Some institutional shareholders seek to exercise influence through direct communication with management and directors.

The stock of most public companies is owned principally by institutional investors. Many retail investors have only indirect interests in public companies through their investments in mutual funds or exchange-traded funds. Under state law, the mutual funds and exchange-traded funds are the shareholders of the companies in which those funds are invested, and the managers of these funds vote the shares of companies owned by the funds. Retail investors in these funds have no direct rights as shareholders of the companies in which the funds have invested. As a result, the influence of retail investors has diminished as the influence of asset managers has increased.

A. DIRECTOR ELECTIONS

Director elections are the principal way in which shareholders influence a corporation. Shareholder influence through director elections can be affected by the term for which directors are elected and the voting standard applicable to director elections. In addition, shareholder influence correlates in part with whether director elections are contested.

1. Term

Directors ordinarily serve for a one-year term that expires at the corporation's next annual meeting of shareholders, with all director nominees standing for election each year. Some companies, however, have "staggered," also known as "classified," boards, with directors divided into classes with staggered terms so that not all directors are elected annually. Typically, staggered boards have three classes, with directors having three-year terms, and one-third of the directors standing for election at each annual shareholder meeting. On the one hand, some companies have maintained that a principal benefit of a staggered board is that it may provide to the board greater continuity than when all directors are elected annually. On the other hand, many shareholders, including most institutional investors, believe a staggered board may inhibit takeovers and that the annual election of directors enhances the board's accountability to shareholders. For this reason, at least for larger corporations, staggered boards are not common. As with most aspects of corporate governance, however, the appropriate approach to director terms will depend on each corporation's specific circumstances.

2. Voting Standards

Under the laws of most states, directors are elected by plurality vote unless a different standard is specified in the certificate of incorporation or bylaws. Plurality voting means that the candidates with the highest number of votes in their favor (even if less than a majority) are elected, up to the maximum number of directorships up for election. A plurality voting standard ensures that a director election is "successful" in the sense that all open directorships are filled, and thus avoids a "failed" election where open directorships are not filled. Plurality voting is the predominant standard used for *contested* elections. Many larger public companies, however, have adopted a majority vote standard for *uncontested* director elections. There are different formulations for majority voting, but, in general, it means that in order to be elected, the number of votes cast in favor of a director candidate's election must exceed the number of votes cast against or withheld from the candidate's election. The rationale behind a majority vote standard is that if a candidate in an uncontested election cannot garner a majority of "favorable" votes, the candidate should not be elected.

If a corporation adopts a majority voting standard for uncontested director elections, a *non-incumbent* director candidate who receives more "against" or "withhold" than "for" votes is not elected. By contrast, because under the law of most states a director serves until a successor is elected, an *incumbent* director who fails to achieve a majority favorable vote in an uncontested election will continue on the board as a "hold over" director. In order to prevent incumbent directors who do not receive the requisite majority vote for reelection from remaining on the board as hold over directors, many companies that have a majority vote standard to elect directors also require incumbent directors who do not receive majority support in an uncontested election to resign or to offer to resign. These director resignation policies often provide that a resignation for failure to receive majority support does not become effective unless accepted by a majority of the members of the board other than the director whose resignation is being considered. Many of these policies also provide a time period and other guidelines for the board to decide whether to accept the resignation.

Some companies retain plurality voting for both contested and uncontested elections but have adopted a director resignation policy for an incumbent director who does not receive majority support in an uncontested election. The combination of plurality voting and a director resignation policy is commonly referred to as a "plurality plus" voting standard.

Regardless of whether a corporation has plurality or majority voting, it is unusual for a director candidate in an uncontested election to receive more against or withhold than for votes. And, in this respect, majority voting does make director elections credible because it is possible that a candidate who does not receive a majority will not be elected or will be required to resign. As a result, many shareholders, including most institutional investors, favor majority voting in director elections because they believe it enhances the board's accountability to shareholders. In addition, as discussed below, a majority voting standard in director elections can make even an uncontested election one that is challenged.

3. Contested Elections

The vast majority of elections for corporate directors are not contested. In a typical election, the board nominates a slate of directors and recommends that the corporation's shareholders vote for the members of that slate; there is usually little doubt that all directors will be elected. There are, however, a number of ways in which a director election can be contested—or at least take on some of the characteristics of a contested election.

The traditional way to wage a contested election is through a proxy contest. Although shareholders have the right under state law to nominate their own candidates, for public companies, it is typically necessary to solicit proxies from other shareholders for such candidates to have any chance of being elected. This solicitation must comply with the SEC's proxy solicitation rules, including the filing and distribution of separate proxy materials. The process can be expensive and time-consuming, and the outcome of a proxy contest is uncertain. Therefore, proxy contests, even contests in which those waging the proxy contest nominate a few directors (a so-called short slate), are not lightly—or very often—undertaken.

Many companies—particularly large publicly traded companies—have adopted proxy access bylaw provisions that provide another opportunity for contested elections. Typically, under proxy access bylaws, shareholders who meet certain requirements (e.g., holding 3 percent of the corporation's outstanding shares for at least three years) have the right to include a limited number of nominees in the corporation's proxy statement. Proxy access provides an opportunity for a contested election without the shareholders needing to file and disseminate separate proxy materials.

Finally, public corporation shareholders can conduct withhold the vote or vote against campaigns in which they urge their fellow shareholders to vote against some or all of the slate of directors nominated by the board. These campaigns are a way for shareholders to express disapproval of board candidates, board oversight, or board policies. Withhold campaigns can be relatively easy and inexpensive for a shareholder to conduct—a formal proxy solicitation is not required, and in some cases all the shareholder does is issue a press release. Withhold campaigns in director elections can have direct consequences at companies with a majority vote standard or with a director resignation policy if the campaign is successful in denying one or more directors a majority favorable vote. Nevertheless, even if all directors are reelected, the issues raised in withhold campaigns can be catalysts for change in board composition, structure, and policies.

B. SHAREHOLDER RELATIONS

Public companies communicate with their shareholders principally through public filings made under U.S. securities laws, at annual shareholder meetings, through investor and analyst calls, and through their websites and social media. U.S. securities laws require companies to file periodic reports containing specified information about the corporation's business operations, financial condition, and performance, as well as to disclose certain material developments in those areas on a current basis. In addition, U.S. securities laws require companies soliciting shareholder votes to provide shareholders with specified information regarding the matters to be voted upon.

Companies may also communicate with shareholders at investor meetings and industry or sector investment conferences. Analysts may ask management to participate in "roadshows" where the corporation's officers are introduced to the analysts' clients. Some companies use videos, podcasts, social media, and corporation websites to communicate with shareholders regarding business, financial, and other matters.

Communications with shareholders of public companies are subject to legal restrictions. In particular, directors must be mindful of the requirements under federal and state securities laws regarding the disclosure of non-public information, including SEC Regulation FD (for fair disclosure). In particular, directors must be careful to avoid selectively disclosing material non-public information to shareholders or potential investors in non-public settings. Public companies typically will publicly file written investor presentations so they are available to all shareholders. In addition, companies will sometimes record and transcribe oral comments made during presentations and earnings calls and make those comments publicly available.

1. Shareholder Engagement by Management

The primary areas of shareholder engagement involve discussions relating to the corporation's financial performance, business operations, and strategy. Management, including the CEO, CFO, or investor relations department, generally handle this engagement through meetings (in person or through electronic media) with investors.

Another area of shareholder engagement involves matters to be voted on at annual shareholder meetings, such as director elections, executive compensation, and shareholder proposals. In addition, although not voted on, disclosures in the corporation's proxy statement regarding governance issues such as board diversity, composition and refreshment, and proxy access are frequently the subject of shareholder engagement. This engagement is typically handled by management, including the corporate secretary and/or investor relations personnel, as well as other subject matter experts.

Oversight by the board or a committee of the board is common. Whether management or a separate department handle investor relations usually depends on the size of the corporation. Larger public companies often have separate investor relations officers or departments, and smaller companies may include investor relations functions within other functions of officers, such as the CEO or CFO, or outside investor relations firms retained by the corporation.

In general, the purpose of the investor relations function is to provide consistent information and messaging about the corporation's operations and financial performance to the investment community. The goal of investor relations is for the corporation's share price to reflect the corporation's fundamental value. Investor relations personnel should know who the corporation's significant investors and equity research analysts are and understand their goals and priorities. Investor relations often determines if investors and analysts may seek or be amenable to specific outreach, coordinate that outreach, and establish a procedure by which communications received from investors and analysts are reviewed and reported to management and the board or a committee of the board.

Investor relations personnel also may be involved in reviewing the corporation's public filings and other communications with shareholders, including the investor relations section of the corporation's website. Both the corporation's website and its proxy statement often disclose the corporation's shareholder engagement policies and goals, the people involved in the corporation's shareholder outreach efforts, and a contact for shareholders to ask questions or raise concerns. The corporation's website and proxy statement also may include disclosure of the nature and extent of specific shareholder outreach efforts.

The amount and timing of shareholder engagement and those involved vary from corporation to corporation. Some companies wait for investors to approach them; others find benefit in proactively seeking meetings with certain shareholders. Companies seeking such meetings may find that the governance professionals of institutional shareholders are more available in the off season than during annual meeting season. As a result, shareholder engagement is often a year-round function.

2. Shareholder Engagement by Directors

Shareholders may wish to engage directly with one or more independent members of the board on any of the subjects noted. For example, institutional shareholders may be concerned about the corporation's operating strategy, management's performance, or strategic alternatives.

They may also wish to discuss topics that are the responsibility of the independent members of the board, such as CEO succession planning, executive compensation, or board composition. Further, as part of their focus on board competence and composition, they may also want to gain first-hand knowledge of the individuals serving on a corporation's board. Some institutional investors expect that a corporation will provide access to its independent directors. Some also expect directors to attend annual shareholder meetings and to be available to answer questions at those meetings.

Companies may have corporate governance guidelines or other policies that address communication by individual board members with shareholders and other third parties. The policies and protocols for director-shareholder engagement best suited to a corporation will depend on many factors, including the nature and extent of existing relationships with investors (including the level of share ownership of the requesting investor), as well as the preferences of investors and directors. Directors should understand the procedures the corporation has in place for communications with shareholders, consult with the corporation's legal department and investor relations personnel about any questions, and make sure any communications are consistent with the policies and procedures.

Meetings or discussions between directors and shareholders usually will be preceded by preparatory meetings or discussions between the officers or directors involved, the legal department, and investor relations personnel. Following any meeting with shareholders, the officers or directors involved will normally report back on the topics discussed, any questions or concerns raised or actions requested, and any necessary follow up. Depending on the extent and importance of the meetings and discussions held, management may prepare a summary and distribute it to the appropriate board committee for information and any follow up.

3. Environmental and Social Issues

Investors are focusing on how the companies in which they invest address environmental and social issues. These issues are often referred to as ESG (environmental, social, and governance), although some institutional investors view governance as separate from environmental and social issues. Environmental and social issues involve a wide range of topics such as human rights policies, environmental impacts, community and political involvement, and sustainability standards both for the corporation and for the corporation's suppliers. Many investors view environmental and social issues as consistent with long-term sustainable value creation and risk mitigation. In addition, industry ratings firms have developed metrics and methodologies for assessing corporation- and industry-specific environmental and social issues, and some investors use these when making investment and voting decisions. Environmental and social issues are often the focus of shareholder proposals submitted to companies for annual meeting voting.

Boards often include relevant environmental and social issues on their agendas. Companies also often report on their websites, in their proxy statements, or in separate sustainability or citizenship reports the environmental and social practices they believe contribute to the corporation's long-term value creation. Some companies have determined that it is appropriate to benchmark the corporation's environmental and social efforts against third-party standards and report publicly on the corporation's progress in meeting those standards.

4. Shareholder Proxy Voting Advisory Firms

Institutional investors who do not have in-house voting policy resources may either rely, to varying degrees, on the recommendations of proxy voting advisory firms regarding how to vote on matters presented at shareholder meetings or work with proxy voting advisory firms to develop customized voting policies. Even institutional investors that do maintain in-house proxy voting teams may subscribe to and consider the voting recommendations of proxy advisory firms.

Shareholder proxy voting advisory firms have policies on a variety of corporate governance items and publish ratings that score a corporation's corporate governance against these policies. Governance items covered include board diversity; executive compensation practices; shareholder rights; audit and risk oversight; and environmental, social, and governance matters. Proxy advisory firms update policies annually based on trends and developments. They may recommend voting against a director or withholding a vote for a director if a corporation's governance is inconsistent with the firm's policy on a particular matter and that director is a member of a board committee responsible for that matter.

Proxy voting advisory firms also provide voting recommendations on shareholder proposals. Moreover, if a shareholder proposal receives the support of a significant percentage of the shares voted but is not implemented or otherwise addressed by the corporation, the shareholder proxy voting advisory firms will often recommend a vote against some or all of the incumbent directors in future elections.

Those responsible for engaging with institutional shareholders should understand which of the corporation's institutional investors rely on shareholder proxy voting advisory firms in determining how to vote. They should also know the criteria applied by the applicable shareholder proxy voting advisory firms in deciding how to vote. In addition, companies may find it beneficial to communicate directly with shareholder proxy voting advisory firms to make sure the corporation information the proxy advisory firms are using is accurate.

5. Activist Investors

One category of institutional investors that receives considerable public attention is the activist investor. These investors look for companies trading at a discount to their fundamental values where there may be opportunities to increase stock prices through share repurchases, spin-offs, capital reallocation, business strategy revisions, or sale transactions. Some activist investors are more aggressive than others. Many have disciplined investment methodologies that are not necessarily short term in nature and rarely engage in the tactics attributed to activist investors, such as public proxy contests. Other such investors have shorter-term investment time horizons and track records of public activism.

Proposals from these investors often focus on causing the corporation to take actions designed to unlock value that the investor believes is not currently reflected in the corporation's share price. Longer-term activist investors sometimes hire their own consultants to study the companies in which they invest and provide those companies with specific recommendations regarding business strategy revisions. Activist investors often invest in companies after a sustained period of lagging stock performance or following significant drops in share price due to negative business developments.

Sometimes these investors will seek board representation. That request may come at the outset or may come only if a corporation resists the investor's other recommendations. In either case, the request for board representation may be combined with a threat to initiate a proxy fight to replace some or all incumbent board members with directors more open to the investor's proposals. Activist investor campaigns for board representation are often resolved through an agreement with the corporation to add one or more directors suggested by the investor to the board, rather than through a proxy contest carried to a final vote.

To be prepared for activist investors, boards of public companies may assemble teams of internal and external advisors, including law, investment banking, proxy solicitation, and investor relations and communication firms. These teams provide boards with periodic briefings on activist investor trends and the corporation's vulnerabilities to and preparedness for activist involvement. Proactively thinking about the corporation from the perspective of an activist investor and having a plan for addressing these investors may assist the board in preparing for engagement with them.

CHAPTER

11 Duties under the Federal Securities Laws

Federal and state laws regulate the disclosure practices and securities transactions of public companies and their directors, officers, and employees. The federal securities laws are administered by the SEC and affect many daily activities of public companies. Violation of these laws may result in significant civil and criminal penalties, imposed not only on the corporation but also potentially on individual directors and officers. Directors need to be particularly attentive to their own, as well as the corporation's, compliance with these laws. Review of programs and policies designed to maintain compliance with the federal securities laws is often delegated to the audit committee or to a committee assigned specific responsibilities for legal compliance.

A corporation must maintain effective systems of internal controls and procedures for collecting, reviewing, and disclosing financial and other material information about the corporation. Quarterly review and certification of the effectiveness of systems and procedures that support SEC filings are required of the CEO and the CFO of public companies. Annual evaluation of internal control over financial reporting by management and attestation of internal control over financial reporting by the external auditor are also required for many companies. The board, generally through its audit committee, should receive and examine reports concerning each of these reviews.

A. SEC REPORTING REQUIREMENTS

Public companies must file both periodic and current reports with the SEC. Periodic reports include an annual report on Form 10-K and quarterly reports on Form 10-Q. Current reports on Form 8-K are required for disclosure of specified significant events and for quarterly earnings releases, material contracts, changes in the board and management, and shareholder meeting voting results. A Form 8-K may also be used for voluntary disclosure of information. The SEC's proxy rules require that the annual meeting proxy statement be accompanied or preceded by an annual report to shareholders. Many of these reports must include specified financial and other information.

The corporation's annual report on Form 10-K contains the last fiscal year's audited financial statements, as well as risk factors, management's discussion and analysis of the corporation's results of operation and financial condition, and important trends and uncertainties. The Form 10-K is the most detailed of the reports filed with the SEC, and it must be signed by a majority of the corporation's directors. Separate and apart from the audit committee's involvement, all directors should review and be satisfied with the corporate processes used to prepare the Form 10-K and understand the significant disclosures in that report. Therefore, the full board should have an opportunity to read, comment on, and ask questions about the Form 10-K before it is filed.

Directors are not expected to verify independently the accuracy of underlying facts contained in earnings releases or reports filed with the SEC, but they should be satisfied that the disclosures are not contrary to the facts as they know them. In addition, the audit committee and the board should be satisfied that there are disclosure controls and procedures in place reasonably designed to achieve the timeliness, accuracy, and completeness of annual and quarterly reports, as well as all other reports and public releases. In addition, the CEO and CFO of public companies are required to review and, based on their knowledge, certify the material accuracy and completeness of quarterly and annual reports. Quarterly assessments of disclosure controls and procedures and annual assessments of internal control over financial reporting are also required. Audit committee members of public companies should be familiar with these certifications and assessments and the procedures undertaken to support them. The audit committee should always be attentive to reports of control deficiencies, especially material weaknesses, and be satisfied with management's classification of items as significant deficiencies rather than as material weaknesses.

B. PROXY STATEMENTS

Public companies soliciting proxies for shareholder votes on the election of directors or other matters must furnish each shareholder with a proxy statement. In most cases, the corporation files only the final proxy statement, as distributed to shareholders. In other cases, if actions other than election of directors or other routine business are to be taken, the corporation must file a preliminary proxy statement with the SEC, which will often review and clear it. Directors should be attentive to the procedures followed in preparing the corporation's proxy statements. It is good practice for every director to review a reasonably close-to-final draft of the proxy statement before it is distributed or filed with the SEC, particularly sections dealing with matters about which the director has personal knowledge or containing a report of a committee on which the director serves. Similar disclosure requirements can apply for corporate action without soliciting proxies.

The proxy statement for the annual shareholder meeting must include information about the corporation's directors, officers, and principal shareholders, as well as about certain of its governance policies. With respect to directors in particular, the proxy statement must include disclosure about each director's and director nominee's experience, qualifications, attributes, or skills that led the board to conclude that the person should serve as a director of the corporation as of the time the proxy statement is filed with the SEC. It must also include extensive information about the corporation's compensation of its officers and directors, in both tabular and narrative form, including a detailed discussion of the corporation's compensation objectives, policies, and practices, as well as information about related person transactions.

C. REGISTRATION STATEMENTS

Directors should take diligent steps to assure the accuracy of their corporation's registration statements filed with the SEC in connection with any offering (including in a merger or acquisition) of the corporation's securities to the public. Regardless of whether a director actually signs the registration statement, the director is liable for any material inaccuracy or omission in the registration statement, including information incorporated by reference from other filed documents, unless the director establishes that, after due diligence, the director was not aware of the inaccuracy or omission.

The director's primary defense to registration statement liability is due diligence. To establish this defense, the director must show that, after reasonable investigation, the director had reasonable grounds to believe and did believe that the registration statement did not contain any materially false or misleading statements or any material omissions that made the registration statement misleading. Actions required by the director to satisfy the due diligence standard will vary with the circumstances. During the registration process, directors should satisfy themselves that the corporation has developed and used appropriate corporate disclosure controls and procedures reasonably designed to ensure the registration statement's accuracy and completeness. Although all registration statements should be prepared with appropriate care, certain registered offerings may have a higher potential for liability, such as an initial public offering, a follow-on equity offering, a large acquisition using the corporation's equity, or a financing or reorganization of a public corporation that has experienced problems. Accordingly, a board meeting or meetings with counsel, accountants, and management present at which there is discussion and analysis of the disclosures in the registration statement should precede the filing of registration statements for such offerings.

For many companies, the disclosures in the corporation's Form 10-K and other reports filed previously with the SEC are incorporated into the registration statement. Therefore, the procedures used to review these reports are important when there is a registered securities offering. Each director should personally review the registration statement for accuracy, with particular attention to those statements and disclosures in the registration statement that are within the director's knowledge and competence. Directors may also want to consider consulting with the corporation's legal counsel to understand any material changes made to disclosure documents in response to SEC comments and to confirm that the process followed is intended to fulfill the due diligence requirements.

D. SALES BY CONTROLLING PERSONS

Unless an exemption is available, the federal securities laws generally require SEC registration of the corporation's securities before those securities can be offered or sold to the public by "controlling persons." (Determining who is a controlling person is a complex question of law and fact for which legal guidance is advisable; directors are often considered to be controlling persons.) The most common exemption for sales in the public trading market is provided by the SEC's Rule 144, which permits the sale of limited amounts of securities without registration if certain conditions are satisfied. Securities acquired by a controlling person in the open market or in a registered offering are subject to the conditions in this rule, which include special filing and disclosure requirements, if they are to be sold to the public. Another exemption sometimes used is private sales that meet requirements similar to those for corporation private offerings.

E. REPORTING SHARE OWNERSHIP AND TRANSACTIONS; SHORT-SWING PROFITS

Certain insiders—directors, executive officers, and more than 10 percent shareholders—of public companies must report to the SEC all their holdings of and transactions in the corporation's equity securities and must disgorge to the corporation any profits realized from buying and selling (or selling and buying) such securities within any six-month period. Any person who becomes such an insider is required to file a report of beneficial ownership and must do so whenever there is a change in beneficial ownership. These reports must be filed on a timely basis. All delinquent filings and filers must be disclosed in the corporation's annual meeting proxy statement, and the delinquencies can trigger monetary fines. An insider is generally deemed to be the owner of securities that are owned by a spouse or child living with the insider and may also be deemed to be the owner of securities held in a trust of which the insider is a trustee, settlor, or beneficiary, or of securities owned by a corporation or other entity controlled by the insider.

Profit disgorgement is required when an insider purchases and sells, or sells and purchases, the corporation's securities within a six-month period. Any such "short-swing profit"—measured as the difference between the prices of any two "matchable" transactions during the six-month period (i.e., the highest-priced sale and the lowest-priced purchase)—must be paid to the corporation. The requirement is intentionally mechanical and, subject to tightly defined regulatory exemptions, applies to all transactions within any six-month period regardless of whether the insider had inside information or, in fact, made a profit on an overall basis. This provision is aggressively enforced by a plaintiffs' bar that monitors SEC filings.

Some transactions, such as the grant and exercise of stock options and the acquisition of securities under employee benefit plans, may be exempt from the purchase and sale triggers of the short-swing profit rules if procedural requirements under SEC rules have been satisfied. Absent an exemption, the receipt of an option, the acquisition of securities through a benefit plan, or the acquisition of a derivative security related to the value of the corporation's common stock is generally considered to be a purchase of the underlying security and could be matchable against a sale. Unexpected liability may result from the application of the short-swing profit rules. For example, other indirect changes in ownership, such as reclassifications, intra-company transactions, pledges, and mergers, may sometimes be considered a purchase or sale transaction for purposes of the short-swing profit rules.

A retiring director may be subject to profit recovery based on transactions occurring during the six months after the director departs. If a director purchases shares of the corporation, resigns, and sells shares within six months after the purchase, liability may be imposed for any short-swing profit even though the individual is no longer a director at the time of the sale.

Directors, officers, and more than 10 percent shareholders also are prohibited from selling short the corporation's shares. As a means to enforce this restriction, they are required to deliver shares against a sale within 20 days.

This regulatory regime is highly technical. It is generally advisable to consult with legal counsel before committing to a transaction in the corporation's securities or in options or other derivatives geared to its securities.

F. INSIDER TRADING

The federal securities laws prohibit corporate insiders, including directors, and the corporation itself from purchasing or selling securities, either on the open market or in private transactions, when they possess non-public, material information about the corporation. The corporation or an insider in possession of such information may not engage in otherwise proscribed securities transactions until the information is publicly disseminated. The corporation should have policies to address securities transactions, including transactions in compensation and retirement plans and gifts of securities. The federal securities laws also prohibit insiders from revealing material, non-public information concerning the corporation, or giving a recommendation to buy or sell based upon such information, to others who trade based upon such information. Under the SEC's Rule 10b5-1, directors and other insiders can mitigate the risk of insider trading liability by adopting plans in advance for scheduled sales and purchases of the corporation's securities. As a general rule, the federal securities laws also prohibit the recipient of a tip ("tippee") from acting on material, non-public information obtained from a corporate source.

Information is material if there is a substantial likelihood that a reasonable investor would consider it important in deciding whether to buy, sell, or hold a security. Some believe that information may be considered material if, upon disclosure, it would likely affect the stock price in a way that favors the insider. If there is any doubt whether undisclosed information is material, legal guidance should be sought or, as a practical alternative, the information should be treated as material.

Violation of any of these insider trading laws triggers strict sanctions. The violator is liable for any profit made or loss avoided. In addition, a court can assess a penalty against the trader, the tipper, or the tippee of treble damages—that is, three times the profits made or losses avoided. Criminal sanctions are also possible. The SEC and the stock exchanges have aggressive programs of discovering and proceeding against insider trading violations. The SEC can award informants who report a violation a percentage of the amount of the penalty recovered. In addition, the SEC can prohibit any individual from serving as an officer or director of any public corporation if the individual has violated the antifraud or insider trading laws and demonstrates unfitness to serve as an officer or director. The misuse of confidential corporate information can also result in violations of directors' duties under state law, leading to civil lawsuits brought by shareholders.

Many public companies have procedures requiring senior executives and directors to contact a designated person before trading in the corporation's securities so that any proposed transaction can be reviewed in light of the current state of public information. Many public companies have policies prohibiting insiders and their affiliates from trading in the corporation's securities during specified "blackout" periods. The board of directors or a committee of the board should periodically review corporate information disclosure and insider trading policies and procedures in view of Regulation FD (discussed next) and insider trading prohibitions.

G. FAIR DISCLOSURE

The SEC's Regulation FD (for fair disclosure) provides that material information about a public corporation may not be disclosed on a selective basis by the corporation or its agents to marketplace participants, such as analysts, brokers, investment advisors, and shareholders who may act on the information and have not agreed to keep the information confidential. Rather, the corporation must take steps to disseminate such information in a manner that makes it broadly available to all market participants simultaneously. As a result, directors should be careful not to disclose non-public information about the corporation and its business. Violations of Regulation FD have resulted in SEC enforcement actions and fines against public companies and corporate officers. Regulation FD has caused public companies to adopt more restrictive policies regarding the persons authorized to speak on behalf of the corporation with securities analysts and others. It has also prompted many companies to make more information public.

H. COMPLIANCE PROGRAMS

Many public companies have established specific policies and procedures dealing with public communications, share ownership reporting, and insider trading. These programs are designed to ensure that the corporation makes complete, accurate, and timely disclosure of material information, complies with the registration requirements, and satisfies other securities law obligations. These programs also help directors and other insiders to comply with insider trading and other applicable laws, and they also help the corporation to meet its obligations under Regulation FD to avoid improper selective disclosure of material information. The audit committee (or a legal affairs committee, if there is one) generally should monitor the establishment and operation of compliance programs.

I. DIRECTORS OF FOREIGN CORPORATIONS

A large number of non-U.S. corporations file reports with the SEC because their securities are traded on U.S. securities markets or they have a large number of U.S. holders. Generally, the federal securities laws require these "foreign private issuers" to file annual reports and other material information distributed to their shareholders with the SEC. In addition, some federal securities laws that involve reporting and corporate governance requirements apply generally to non-U.S. corporations that have securities registered with the SEC. The SEC, in adopting these laws, has considered the concerns of foreign private issuers and made some rules inapplicable to them or included special provisions addressing their concerns. Directors of foreign private issuers should be aware of the general categories of substantive corporate governance requirements that may apply to their corporations.

CHAPTER 12

Liabilities, Indemnification, and Insurance

Directors may incur personal liability for breaches of their duty of care or their duty of loyalty or for failure to satisfy other legal or regulatory requirements, including the federal securities laws. Corporations may provide for limitations on these potential liabilities, and may also provide directors (and officers) with indemnification rights and insurance against liabilities and litigation expenses. These provisions allow directors to focus on performing their duties without undue personal liability exposure. Directors should periodically review the corporation's indemnification and insurance protections as applicable to both directors and officers.

A. SOURCES OF LIABILITY

1. Corporate Law Liability

As noted earlier, directors have two primary functions: decision making and oversight. Corporate law generally provides that, in performing these functions, directors are fiduciaries and therefore have both a duty of care and a duty of loyalty. Directors may in theory be liable for violating either of these duties, but nearly all public corporations formed in U.S. jurisdictions have, through their charters, precluded monetary liability for directors who breach only the duty of care. Directors should inquire about the extent to which the corporation has eliminated such liability.

Directors in most jurisdictions may, however, be subject to monetary liability for breaching the duty of loyalty. For example, directors may incur liability when they have a conflicting personal interest or are dominated or controlled by a person or entity with such a conflict. Directors should be alert to such conflicts, particularly in corporations with controlling shareholders and in change-in-control transactions—where courts are especially sensitive to compliance with the duty of loyalty. There are several measures available to directors to address these concerns, including disclosure of potential conflicts, recusal of conflicted directors, use of independent committees and advisors, and shareholder votes. In addition to liability involving a conflict of interest, directors may also incur liability for breach of the duty of loyalty when their inattention to their duties rises to a level constituting bad faith or conscious disregard for their duties. Thus, it is important for directors to be actively engaged in discussions and deliberations after having gathered relevant information for board action. Good recordkeeping of board procedure and deliberations is important in protecting directors from liability, especially when, in retrospect, business decisions with poor outcomes can appear to have resulted from conflicts or inattention.

In addition to liability for breach of duties, directors may also be personally liable for authorizing dividends or other distributions, such as stock repurchases, when a corporation is insolvent. This area requires particular caution, as directors may be liable for even simple negligence—a lower standard than that typically applicable to liability for breaching fiduciary duties. Accordingly, whenever there is any question as to a corporation's solvency, directors should obtain appropriate financial and legal advice before making distributions to shareholders. The subjects for advice may include requesting and receiving a certificate of the chief financial officer or an independent opinion as to the corporation's compliance with the applicable solvency or other requirements for making a distribution.

2. Federal Securities Law Liability

Directors may also be personally liable under the federal securities laws—in some cases even when they act in good faith. In certain circumstances, negligence, by itself, is sufficient to establish liability. In other situations, liability may be imposed, subject only to due diligence or other defenses, without a finding of fault or intent to deceive.

3. Liability under Other Laws

Directors may also be subject to personal liability under other state and federal statutes, such as antitrust, workplace safety, and environmental laws. Good faith and careful monitoring of management programs directed toward corporate legal compliance (including periodic briefings on the timely and proper functioning of compliance programs and any changes in them) should provide substantial safeguards against any such personal liability.

B. PROTECTIONS

As noted above, several measures help to protect directors from personal liability: charter provisions limiting liability, rights to indemnification, advancement of related expenses, and insurance.

1. Limitation of Liability

Most state corporation statutes permit a corporation's charter to include a provision eliminating or limiting the liability of directors to the corporation and its shareholders for monetary damages resulting from breaches of certain duties. These provisions most frequently eliminate exposure to claims by the corporation or by shareholders (either directly or derivatively on behalf of the corporation) for monetary damages for breaches of the duty of care under the law of the jurisdiction under which the corporation is formed. These provisions do not, however, cover claims for injunctive or other non-monetary relief or liabilities to third parties, and they do not protect a director from liabilities resulting from violations of federal law or laws of foreign nations or states other than the corporation's jurisdiction of incorporation. Generally, depending on the language of these provisions, they do not protect directors from monetary liability for illegal dividends or stock repurchases, actions or omissions in bad faith, breach of the duty of loyalty, intentional violations of law, or actions when the director received an improper benefit.

2. Indemnification

Most state corporation statutes specify the circumstances in which the corporation is permitted to indemnify directors against liability and to pay or advance related reasonable expenses incurred in defending claims arising from their service as directors.

In general, directors must meet a certain standard of conduct before being indemnified. The standard for permissible indemnification in many state statutes is that the individual director must have acted in good faith and with a reasonable belief that the director's conduct was in (or not opposed to) the best interests of the corporation. In the case of a criminal proceeding, the director must also have had no reasonable cause to believe the conduct was unlawful. These statutes give corporations the power to indemnify directors in actions by third parties, including class actions, for expenses (including attorneys' fees), judgments, fines, and amounts paid in settlement. In some instances, however, indemnification is not permitted, even if the director has complied with applicable standards of conduct. For example, many jurisdictions prohibit indemnification for liability in derivative actions, unless ordered by a court.

3. Advance for Expenses

In addition to permitting indemnification, state corporation statutes generally permit a corporation to pay a director's legal expenses during the pendency of most lawsuits before final disposition of the proceeding. The cost of defending a claim may be substantial, making advance of expenses important. A director benefiting from such an advance, however, must promise to repay the advance if it is ultimately determined that the director is not entitled to indemnification.

4. Mandatory Indemnification and Advance for Expenses

Many state statutes provide that indemnification for legal expenses is mandatory when (or to the extent that) the director is successful in defending a suit. In order to induce directors to serve, most corporations provide for mandatory indemnification and advancement of expenses under additional circumstances through provisions in their charters or bylaws or through separate agreements with directors. In many instances, these provisions provide that directors are to be indemnified and advanced expenses to the fullest extent permitted by law. In other cases, the indemnification rights are more limited. Directors should understand the extent of their mandatory rights and any limits on those rights.

5. Indemnification Agreements

Many corporations and their directors and officers enter into contracts to indemnify and advance expenses to them. These indemnification agreements are increasingly common and perform three functions. First, they are a contract that is enforceable against the corporation and, thus, give the indemnitee a right to sue the corporation for breach of contract, in addition to any other right the indemnitee may have under state law or a charter or bylaw provision. Second, they often expand the scope of indemnification to the maximum extent permitted by applicable law, including so-called non-exclusivity provisions of some state corporation statutes that permit corporations to indemnify and advance expenses beyond the limits specifically required or permitted by statute. It is generally thought that the extent of these provisions is limited by "public policy," although there is no clear definition of what public policy would be in this regard. Third, indemnification agreements usually set forth various procedures for seeking and requiring the corporation to make indemnification and expense payments. Typically, the law of the state of incorporation governs the indemnification agreement.

6. Insurance

Most corporations purchase directors and officers (D&O) liability insurance covering (1) the corporation for. any payment of indemnification and advances for expenses and (2) directors and officers, if the corporation is unwilling to pay indemnification or expense advance obligations (perhaps because of a change in control) or is unable to pay such obligations (perhaps because of insolvency or because the claim is one for which indemnification or advancement is not permitted). The relevant statutes in most jurisdictions permit the corporation to pay premiums for this insurance. Because of uncertainty regarding the right of directors and officers to access policies that also cover the corporation, corporations should consider policies that cover only non-management directors. Such policies often include terms more favorable to the insured (for example, no deductible) than policies that cover both the corporation and its directors.

Certain areas of activity, such as environmental, employee benefit, or antitrust matters, are often excluded from coverage under a typical D&O policy. Sexual misconduct–related claims may be excluded under some D&O policies, especially if they involve not only verbal but also physical harassment or assault. Coverage may also exclude conditions in existence at the time of the application for insurance. D&O insurance generally does not cover fraud, fines, insider trading, and other criminal penalties, and it sometimes excludes punitive damages.

Insurance coverage is not available in every case. Most policies are written on a "claims made" (as compared to an "occurrence") basis, covering only defined claims lodged against directors during a specified period. In addition, the terms of coverage under differing policies are complex and may vary from insurer to insurer. Moreover, insurance markets change rapidly, and insurers may assert numerous reservations or defenses when claims are made. Therefore, directors are well advised to engage experts with knowledge and experience in current market conditions.

In short, it is important for directors to understand the scope of the corporation's D&O insurance on a continuing basis. Many boards require an annual presentation to directors on insurance coverage. Directors should ascertain the level of expertise of the person within the corporation responsible for negotiating the coverage or, in the alternative, determine whether an outside expert, familiar with current market conditions and policy and claim issues, is assisting in the process. Directors should also take care (as is true in the case of any insurance policy) in completing policy applications and questionnaires and inquire about the insurance carrier's reputation for handling insurance claims and its financial strength. These considerations may be as or more important than premium pricing. Disputes with the insurance carrier over coverage when litigation materializes are an unwanted and costly distraction. D&O insurance is a complex area, and directors should seek assurance that the corporation's coverage does in fact afford the best protection obtainable in the current marketplace. Finally, directors should inquire whether coverage extends beyond their term of service.